MW01534902

ON THE STUDY OF CHASIDUS

A Trilogy of Chasidic Essays

ON THE STUDY OF CHASIDUS

A Trilogy of Chasidic Essays

Some Aspects of Chabad Chasidism
On the Teachings of Chasidus
On Learning Chasidus

by
RABBI YOSEF YITZCHAK SCHNEERSOHN
OF LUBAVITCH
זצוקללה"ה נבג"מ זי"ע

•

Translated by
Rabbi Nissan Mindel
Rabbi Zalman Posner

Published by
KEHOT PUBLICATION SOCIETY
770 Eastern Parkway • Brooklyn, New York 11213

5757 • 1997

ON THE STUDY OF CHASIDUS
A Trilogy of Chasidic Essays
Copyright © 1997
by
Kehot Publication Society
770 Eastern Parkway / Brooklyn, New York 11213
(718) 774-4000 / FAX (718) 774-2718
E-Mail: merkos@chabad.org

Order Department:
291 Kingston Avenue / Brooklyn, New York 11213
(718) 778-0226 / FAX (718) 778-4148

ISBN 0-8266-0438-2

Formerly published under the titles:
Some Aspects of Chabad Chasidism
On the Teachings of Chasidus
On Learning Chasidus

Printed in the United States of America

Rabbi Yosef Yitzchak Schneersohn
זצוקללה"ה נבג"מ זי"ע

TABLE OF CONTENTS

FOREWORD TO THE NEW TRILOGY EDITION

In the 1940's and 50's, English readers had little access to the vast wealth of Chasidic literature. To fill this void, several fundamental works were selected for adaptation into English. Since the importance of studying Chasidus was not then widely understood, three short essays on this subject, all authored by the sixth Lubavitcher Rebbe, Rabbi Yosef Yitzchak Schneersohn, were among those first chosen:

Some Aspects of Chabad Chasidism, translated by Rabbi Dr. Nissan Mindel, based on a letter of the Previous Rebbe, published in *Igrot Kodesh* Vol. 3, 672ff;

On the Teachings of Chasidus, translated by Rabbi Zalman Posner, entitled in the original Hebrew, *Kuntres Torat HaChasidus*;

On Learning Chasidus, also translated by Rabbi Zalman Posner, entitled in the original, *Kuntres Limud HaChasidus*.

Since earlier editions are no longer in print, and there is continued demand for these publications, a new, slightly revised, edition of all three is hereby presented.

The current edition, edited by Rabbi Y. Eliezer Danzinger, and prepared for publication by Rabbi Yosef B. Friedman, also contains chapter titles for *On the Teachings of Chasidus*, adapted into English by the editor, from the original Hebrew. These titles were composed by the Rebbe, Rabbi Menachem M.

Schneerson, at the request of his father-in-law, Rabbi Yosef Yitzchak Schneersohn.

The Translator's Explanatory Notes, which appeared at the beginning of the earlier individual editions, have been included in the appendices of this collective edition. Readers are encouraged to refer to these Notes, as they will undoubtedly help clarify many of the terms appearing in the essays. The Brief Biography, which appeared in the earlier editions of *Some Aspects of Chabad Chasidism*, appears in the appendices, as well.

Kehot Publication Society
Brooklyn, New York
18th of *Elul*, 5757

Book One

SOME ASPECTS OF CHABAD CHASIDISM

Translator's Foreword
to the First Edition (1944)

SOME ASPECTS OF CHABAD CHASIDISM is published here for the first time in English. It has been previously published in Hebrew, Yiddish and German It is a translation of a letter written some time ago[1] by the sixth Lubavitcher Rebbe, Rabbi Yosef Yitzchak Schneersohn [of sainted memory], to one of his noted correspondents, in reply to a query: Would the study of Chabad Chasidus bring practical results to that type of intellectual Jew who, though previously estranged from Judaism, has become conscious of a desire to return to his people and to learn something of his spiritual heritage.

In view of the fact that *Chabad*, meaning *wisdom*, *understanding* and *knowledge*, claims to be an intellectual study of Judaism, the correspondent in question asked how the study of *Chabad* could best serve this type of intellectual Jew.

For the sake of the layman, the translation of the letter above referred to, has in many instances been simplified, with the author's permission, so as to make it not too difficult for the novice to understand.

Nissan Mindel

---

1. 1936. The full text appears in *Igrot Kodesh*, vol. 3, pp. 672ff.

Publisher's Preface
to the Second Edition (1957)

THE FIRST EDITION having been totally exhausted, and in view of the continued demand for this publication, a second edition is presented herewith.

Since the first edition was published, Rabbi Yosef Yitzchak Schneersohn, of sainted memory, passed away. The Biographical Sketch has accordingly been brought up-to-date. A list of his published works (still incomplete), appears in his Short Biography, published by **Kehot Publication Society** in 5708 (1947).

Machne Israel, Inc.
Publishers

4

CHAPTER ONE

WE ALL KNOW that man has a soul which distinguishes him from all other animals and which marks him as the choice of the entire Creation. This soul, which is a *part* of G-d, descends to earth by the will of G-d to vitalize the human being, enabling him to fulfill the purpose for which he is created.

The purpose of the soul's descent is to enable man to serve the Creator, for man's own benefit, as well as for the benefit of the surrounding world. A Jew can fulfill this purpose only by accepting the Divine Rule and fulfilling the commandments and precepts that G-d gave us on Mount Sinai.

Thus the religion of Israel is a Divine gift, and as such it is, in many aspects, far beyond the grasp of such terrestrial beings as humans. However, the fact that we cannot fully understand all aspects of our religion does not affect the bond that exists between us and our G-d. For every Jew possesses an innate feeling which places his relationship to G-d on the level of that which exists between child and father. Indeed, it is written:[1] בנים אתם לה׳ אלקיכם "You are children unto G-d your G-d!"

Just as a child, who does not know at all how and why that particular man is its father, and that particular woman is its mother, is still drawn to them by an inner feeling of love and devotion, so are the Jewish people G-d's children, imbued with an instinctive awareness that G-d is our strength and our life.

---

1. Deut. 14:1.

5

This inner feeling is expressed in the words:[2]
שמע ישראל ה׳ אלקינו ה׳ אחד – *Hear, O Israel, G-d is our G-d, G-d is One.* A Jew feels (Hear, O Israel) that G-d is our strength (G-d is our G-d אלקינו), He Who is the One and Only Creator (G-d is One).[3]

This Divine instinctive feeling is alive in every Jew, from the greatest of the great to the most ignorant in Torah knowledge.

This is one of the fundamental principles expounded at length by the founder of Chabad Chasidus, the Alter Rebbe, Rabbi Schneur Zalman of Liadi.[4]

---

2. Deut. 6:4.
3. *Shema* also means understand, feel, and *Elokim* implies strength.
4. 5505–5573 (1745–1812); author of the *Tanya*, etc.

CHAPTER TWO

THE RELATIONSHIP BETWEEN Israel and G-d through the medium of our religion is explained in the *Zohar*[1] as follows:

> *Three are interlocked together: Israel, the Torah and the Holy One, blessed be He, and all are on different planes, one higher than the other, partly hidden, partly revealed.*

The meaning of this saying is that the three—Israel, Torah and G-d—are linked together like a chain of three rings. The upper part of the bottom ring is held by the lower part of the middle ring, and the upper part of the middle ring is held by the lower part of the top ring.

In each of the three rings there is a hidden part, and a disclosed part. Similarly, there are apparent qualities and latent qualities in each of the three: Israel, the Torah and G-d.

Among the apparent qualities of Israel may be mentioned the intelligence and inherent character of the Jew, in the very nature of which he is distinguished from other peoples.

To the latent qualities of Israel belong the original and hidden intellect lying in the very depth of the soul, and the pure, simple and refined faith (alive at the bottom of the heart of every Jew), in the One and only Creator.

As to the Torah, the part that is apparent is to be found in the logical interpretation of all the subjects of the Torah,

---

1. Compare *Zohar* III, 73a.

embracing not merely all interests of man, from his very birth until his last breath, even to the manner of his return to the earth whence he came, but also a full account of the Creation and the progress of the world.

The latent part of the Torah, on the other hand, lies in its Divine intellect, which differs essentially from the human intellect, and therefore cannot be fathomed.

CHAPTER THREE

AS IN THE case of Israel and the Torah, so in the case of G-d, there are the apparent or conceivable attributes, and the hidden or inconceivable attributes.

What is *conceivable* of the Divine Being is that He creates and forms the universe and the creatures. Creating them from nothing, He constantly vitalizes them, as it is written:[1] *He who in His goodness each day, constantly renews the work of the Creation.* This means that G-d continuously renews the existence of the world and all creatures, creating and forming them from nothing every moment. In other words, the act of creation is *continuous*, repeating itself in the same way as in the beginning of creation.

David, King of Israel, recognizes 'Him that spoke and there was the world' by observing Nature, as he frequently exclaimed,[2] *How great are Your deeds!*, or,[3] *How many are Your deeds!* In Psalms, he teaches us wisdom, understanding and insight to recognize in nature and in its beauty—its Creator, our Father and King, blessed be His Name. By this recognition King David is moved to a sense of admiration for the Creator and devotion to Him, which he expresses so inspiringly in the holy Psalms. And this is the secret of our prayers, which are in part composed of Psalms—the soul's expression of yearning and desire to cleave to the Master of all the Universe, the source of all life.

---

1. Daily morning prayers.
2. Psalms 92:6.
3. Ibid. 104:24.

What is *inconceivable* about the Divine Being is the essence and entity of the supreme Creator, and what lies beyond the point of *Life creating life*, as it has been said,[4] "It is not the essence of the Divine Being that He creates worlds and creatures, and sustains them."

It is written:[5] *From my flesh I behold G-d.* Man consists of body and soul. Just as the soul fills and vitalizes the whole body, so does G-d fill and vitalize the whole world. But can we say that the *entire* essence and function of the soul is that it sustains the body? Similarly, we cannot say that the entire essence of G-d is that He creates and sustains the world and all its creatures. Here lies a great deal that is inconceivable to the human mind. Nonetheless, the realization of G-d's greatness must move us to a longing and yearning to cleave to the Creator of all things.

---

4. *Torah Or, Megillat Esther*, 166a.
5. Job 19:26.

CHAPTER FOUR

THIS IS THE gist of the *Zohar* quoted above: *Three are interlocked together, Israel, the Torah and the Holy One blessed be He, and all are on different planes, one higher than the other, partly hidden and partly revealed.*

Israel, Torah and G-d are joined together into complete union, as it is said: "The Holy One blessed be He, the Torah and Israel are all one," and their union comes about through the revealed and hidden qualities of each of them, mentioned above.

However, the way that they unite is two-fold:

a) The revealed qualities of Israel unite with the revealed attributes of G-d, by means of the revealed part of the Torah; and the latent qualities of Israel unite with the latent attributes of G-d, by means of the latent part of the Torah.

b) The revealed qualities of Israel are connected with the hidden qualities of Israel, and the hidden qualities of Israel in turn unite with the revealed part of the Torah; the revealed part of the Torah is connected with its hidden part, and this in turn unites with the revealed attributes of G-d; finally, the revealed attributes of G-d are connected with His hidden attributes and thus the union is completed.

These two manners of uniting share a common feature: both tend to reveal the concealed, but create nothing new. For the three rings mentioned above are essentially interlocked even when not revealed.

CHAPTER FIVE

IT FOLLOWS THAT this union with G-d exists in every Jew, man or woman, young or old, whether learned in the Torah or ignorant of it. At the same time, however, various factors influence the feeling of this union, either strengthening it or weakening it.

This will be understood by an example: Two men, one of whom is deaf, are walking in a busy street. The deaf person does not hear the honking of the cars or the exclamations of the drivers, but the healthy person does. However, if the noise of the traffic becomes overwhelming, the healthy person, too, is deafened by the noise and hears no better than the deaf fellow. On the other hand, the deaf person, too, can notice signs and feel the actual touch of objects around him.

The tumult of worldly material life deafens the ears of reason and dulls the senses of the brain and heart. This is particularly true of youth born amid wealth, and raised in a life devoid of Torah and religion. In them and their like the bonds of spiritual attachment are broken: their ears become deaf to the word of G-d, to observing the practical precepts; their eyes are closed to the beauty of G-d's Torah.

Two circumstances may motivate a person to do teshuvah (to repent and return to G-d): a) abundant good, or b) crushing poverty. Nowadays, the cause of religious reawakening is, to our regret and misfortune, very bitter, but the effect—the return to G-d, to His religion and Torah—is sweet. This awakening demonstrates that the Jewish heart is alive, and the soul of the Jewish nation is perfectly intact.

CHAPTER SIX

ONE OF THE spiritual diseases of our generation is the habitual neglect of simplicity, and the preference for so-called enlightenment and superficial brilliance.

To be sure, the sons and daughters of Israel, of the enlightened and educated classes are now eager to return to our religion and Torah, but they long for the dewy brilliance of wisdom, discernment and insight of religion, which alone, in their opinion, could saturate and satisfy their souls and bring about their spiritual revival.

But the real truth is that true revival lies in the fulfillment of the practical precepts—such as Shabbat observance, family sanctity, *kashrut*, putting on *tefillin*, etc.—and in stirring up one's consciousness, lying dormant at the bottom of one's heart, to the love of G-d, the love of Torah, and the love of fellow Jews.

It would be extremely beneficial if the spiritual leaders were to devote special articles in books and periodicals, to teach those who desire to return to the right path, which, as stated, lies in the fulfillment of the practical precepts, observing and practicing them with simplicity, like the rest of the sons and daughters of Israel.

Thus the main task of Jewish scholars and Rabbis everywhere is to bring about the realization that the essential aspect of Judaism is observance of the practical precepts.

One of the things that offer spiritual pleasure and delight is the sight of a beautiful painting. We all know that the most talented artist is the one who can ably express a simple, natural scene such as a corn-field playing in the breeze, or the sight of sea-waves, or the setting of the sun and rising of the moon upon a wide landscape crossed by a stream. In all such scenes the Creator implanted a simple, natural beauty and a wonderful splendor.

So it is also with regard to the worship of G-d. Sincere worship, by observing the precepts with simplicity, is dearer than all the worthiest cultures and ideologies.

CHAPTER SEVEN

MANY STORIES AND scores of Chasidic traditions which came down to us from generation to generation about the saintly Rabbi Israel Baal Shem Tov, the first exponent of general Chasidus; about his disciple, the Maggid (Preacher) of Mezeritch; and about my saintly ancestor, the Alter Rebbe, Rabbi Schneur Zalman of Liadi, founder of Chabad Chasidus— their saintly memory be blessed, and may their virtues be ever a shield unto us and all Israel—testify to their extraordinary love of simplicity and sincerity in the Divine worship of the Jew.

A story is told about the Rebbe, author of *"Tzemach Tzedek"*[1] who was a famous *gaon*[2] in *Shass*[3] and *posekim*,[4] and who was versed in the books of Kabbalah and the writings of the *Ari*:[5]

All night the *"Tzemach Tzedek"* had studied, and at dawn he stood up to pray. It was in the month of *Sivan*, and he was fasting. After spending some hours in devout prayer, he sat down to resume his study, still wrapped in his *tallit* and *tefillin*.

That same day, which was a market day, two Jewish residents of a village near Lubavitch, Benjamin-Bainush and Isaac-Saul, came to town. Both were rather ordinary men, but very pious; and they traveled together in same wagon.

---

1. Rabbi Menachem Mendel Schneersohn, 1789–1866, third leader of Chabad.
2. Highest title accorded to a Talmudist.
3. The entire Talmud.
4. Codifiers of Jewish law.
5. Rabbi Isaac Luria, renowned 16th Century Kabbalist.

Benjamin-Bainush soon sold his merchandise, and the day being long yet, went to the synagogue to wait for Isaac-Saul, who, after selling his wares, would be passing that street in his wagon and would, of course, turn into the synagogue for the *mincha* (afternoon) service. Afterwards they would ride home together.

On entering the synagogue, Benjamin-Bainush, a man of no learning, drew out a book of Psalms from his coat pocket, and began reciting the Psalms in a touching voice.

The saintly Rebbe, sitting wrapped up in his *tallit* and *tefillin* engrossed in study, soon perceived the voice reciting the Psalms, a voice coming from the depth of the heart, touching the very soul. The Rebbe turned to see who it was—Benjamin-Bainush, the villager. The Rebbe was moved to tears, envying the sincerity and simplicity of Benjamin-Bainush, an ignorant villager.

Just then Efraim Yoffe of Kopust entered, one of the most prominent Chasidim of the Rebbe's father-in-law, the Mitteler Rebbe, Rabbi DovBer.[6] The Rebbe said to the newcomer: "I wish that I could recite even one verse of the Psalms with the simplicity and sincerity of Reb Benjamin-Bainush."

How true are the words of the Psalmist:[7] *The L-rd is near to all who call unto Him, to all who call unto Him in truth.*

---

6. Son of the Alter Rebbe, 1773-1827, second leader of Chabad.

7. Psalms 145:18.

CHAPTER EIGHT

THE ALTER REBBE, founder of Chabad Chasidus, states that the main objective of Chasidus is to mold one's character. In other words, the essence of man's service must be concentrated on himself—to mold his own character.

Chabad Chasidus is a comprehensive discipline, arranged in perfect order—in its own style—into a number of elementary, fundamental and principle books, written by the founders of Chabad Chasidus, each *Nassi*[1] in his generation.

The first Chasidim, the disciples of the Alter Rebbe, were men eminent in the wisdom of the Torah and in piety, outstanding theologians, and gifted with remarkable intellects. It was to them that the saintly Alter Rebbe expounded the principles and doctrines of Chasidus.

---

1. The head of Chabad is called *Nassi*, prince or leader, by the Chasidim.

CHAPTER NINE

IN THOSE DAYS, these disciples were selflessly devoted to the study of Divine wisdom. They spent many hours of the day, many days—often the nights—of the week, and many weeks and months during the year, in seclusion.

They did not consider this seclusion as anything in the nature of self-torture or sorrowful castigation. On the contrary, it was a source of special pleasure to them, from which they derived great spiritual joy and delight. For in it and through it they were not merely escaping the earthly material swamp, but were ascending the path leading to perfect purity, in order to perceive the light of G-d with a clear intellect and conception.

Among these disciples were several of a unique type, who were divorced from earthly and corporeal matters. For all their being, spirit and soul, was devoted to striving to ascend the Mount of G-d, and to reaching the highest peak.

These unique and outstanding men, though few in number, exercised considerable influence on the disciples of lower stature, to the extent of it becoming proverbial—even among the mediocre students—that the object of man is the domination of spirit over matter, i.e. the mastery of idealism over materialism.

This adage, *the domination of spirit over matter*, does not present a defined task, but varies according to one's standing and station. Nevertheless, it clearly indicates that every person must strive to attain a higher standard, and should yearn and strive to rise, step by step, in thought, word and deed, in the acquisition of the highest virtues, and the attainment of spiritual perfection.

This motto won thousands upon thousands of men and women of all ranks of the Jewish people, into the camp of the Chasidim.

CHAPTER TEN

THE DOCTRINES OF Chasidus, in general, and of Chabad-Chasidus in particular, are nothing but an explanation of, and clear indication to, the meaning of the verse, *All the earth is full of His Glory*,[1] based on two principles:

a) Everything is the Divine Being, and b) the Divine Being is everything.

The principles of Chasidus teaches that: There is no space devoid of Him and no thought can conceive Him. Chabad Chasidus extends these principles by explaining at great length and expounding with the aid of abundant empirical examples, what is meant by "there is no space devoid of Him." Furthermore, it teaches that though "no thought can conceive Him," nevertheless, it is the duty of man to seek enlightenment in the wisdom of G-d, and to understand and conceive it to the best of his intelligence, as it is written:[2]

You shall know this day and reflect in your heart that the Lord is G-d, in the heavens above and upon the earth below; there is no other.

In the course of ten years since the first disciples left the study hall of the Alter Rebbe, and settled in various districts all over the country, each man in his vicinity had set up a lighthouse, spreading the light of Chabad Chasidus, teaching the Jewish people to serve G-d in a spirit of intelligent recognition and conception.

---

1. Isaiah 6:3.
2. Deut. 4:39.

Those Chasidim taught as well as practiced the word of G-d according to the teachings of Chasidus, which was their guide in daily life.

CHAPTER ELEVEN

ONE WHO IS acquainted with the history and life of the Jews in Russia, Poland and Vohlyn in those days, knows of the pure religious sincerity that shone so brightly in the Jewish home. Everything connected with Shabbat observance and the practice of precepts—not to mention such matters as faith in G-d, and love for the Torah and its *mitzvot*—was practiced by them with great warmth and with an absolutely selfless devotion.

It is not surprising, therefore, that as soon as the doctrines of Chabad Chasidus were publicized, its students and exponents—those noted Chasidim—exercised a great influence even on those whose intelligence could not grasp the Chasidic philosophy, but who became attached to practical Chasidus—"the domination of spirit over matter"—with all their heart, soul and being, and with utter self-sacrifice.

This selfless devotion of the Chasidim to Chasidus effected—not merely among the Chasidim of heart and intellect, but even among the practical Chasidim—the emergence of new features in their character, with an inner glow and vitality, which they passed on to their children from generation to generation.

The Chasidic community grew and struck roots among a broad cross-section of our people, and forty years after the Alter Rebbe founded Chabad Chasidus (5534–5574; 1774–1814), his son, DovBer, the Mitteler Rebbe, wrote Chasidic discourses in the spoken language—Yiddish.

CHAPTER TWELVE

THE VOLUMES ON Chabad Chasidus of the first three generations reflect the growth of the Chasidic community and its firm foot-hold among our people:

Some of his printed works[1] on Chasidus of the first generation and its *Nassi* the Alter Rebbe:

1. *Likkutei Amarim* (Gleanings of Lectures), or *Tanya*;
2. *Torah Or* (Torah-Light);
3. *Likkutei Torah* (Torah Gleanings);
4. *Be'urei HaZohar* (Commentaries to the *Zohar*);
5. *Siddur* (Prayer Book, Commentaries, in 2 volumes).

The second generation and its *Nassi*: the Mitteler Rebbe. Some of his printed works:

1. *Imrei Binah* (Sayings of Wisdom);
2. *Pirush HaMilot* (Commentaries on the Prayers);
3. *Torat Chaim* (Law of Life);
4. *Shaar HaEmunah* (The Gate of Faith);
5. *Shaar HaYichud* (The Gate of Unity);
6. *Shaarei Orah* (The Gates of Light);
7. *Shaarei Teshuva* (The Gates of Penitence, 2 volumes);
8. *Derech HaChaim* (The Path of Life);
9. *Kuntres HaHitpaalut* (A Tract on Ecstasy);
10. *Pokeach Ivrim* (Opening the eyes of the Blind)—in Yiddish.

---

1. The lists printed here have since grown and greatly expanded to include hundreds of volumes.

The third generation and its *Nassi*: the *"Tzemach Tzedek"*. Some of his printed works on Chasidus:

1. *Derech Mitzvotecha* (The Path of Your Commandments);
2. *Derech Emunah* (The Path of Faith);
3. *Or HaTorah* (The Light of the Torah).

During the 158 years since the appearance of the first work—*Tanya*—as an open writ to all the Chasidim, the teachings of Chabad Chasidus spread throughout the world by means of various *maamarim* (Chasidic discourses). However, the study of Chasidus requires preliminary training and preparation in piety and in the practice of the precepts, which is the foundation of the Torah, and the basis of existence of the Jewish people.

CONCLUSION

THE THEORETICAL ASPECTS of Chabad Chasidus form a systematic study, explaining that *all the earth is full of His glory*. Whoever is gifted with intellect and reason can learn it. The wisdom of Chabad, however, can only be acquired after suitable preparation in the service of G-d and the practice of *mitzvot*. For Chabad Chasidus, like Chasidus in general, is the soul of our Torah and religion. There can be no soul without a body, and the body is—the performance of the religious precepts.

As any intellectual study, the study of Chabad Chasidus can be taken up anywhere and at any time. It depends solely upon the intellect and the heart of the teacher and student. But the primary perequisite for this study, both for teacher and student, is an adequate preparation in the performance of the *mitzvot*, which is as necessary to the understanding of Chabad as soil and light are vital to the flourishing rose.

Unquestionably, the study of Chabad Chasidus would be of great benefit to those who would devote themselves to learn it. However, each art and science demands the fulfillment of certain conditions before it can be fully mastered.

It is the sacred task of the Rabbis and Torah scholars everywhere to bring to the realization of the Jewish intelligentsia, that true return to G-d means observing *mitzvot*, such as keeping Shabbat and Holidays, observing family sanctity, eating kosher food, putting on *tefillin*, etc., and that the main thing about this practice is to observe with simplicity and sincerity. For this simplicity and sincerity have always attested to the beauty, perfection and stoutness of the heart of the Jewish Nation.

* * *

May our G-d, G-d of our fathers, Guardian of His people Israel, enlighten our intellect and awaken our heart, and the hearts of all the sons and daughters of Israel, to serve Him sincerely and devotedly and to observe His commandments. May He hasten our Redemption through Mashiach, the Righteous Redeemer, speedily in our days. Amen.

Book Two

ON THE TEACHINGS OF CHASIDUS

Translator's Foreword to the First Edition

EASTERN EUROPEAN JEWRY in the eighteenth century had not yet recovered from the ravages of the pogroms of 1648–1649. The people were depressed spiritually and impoverished materially. Ignorance and despondency (the latter caused by the former) deadened the spirit of the people; they had no life in this world and could expect little better in the Hereafter.

Rabbi Israel Baal Shem Tov embarked on the ambitious program of elevating the spirit of the Jews, teaching them, encouraging them to serve G-d with sincerity and joy, emphasizing the homely virtues of the simple folk. His efforts met with conspicuous success. Countless thousands turned to him and Chasidus—as his new movement was called—for spiritual sustenance. It was no less than a major renaissance of the Jewish spirit.

As might be expected, opponents were not lacking. Opposition concentrated primarily in Lithuania, the center of Talmudic scholarship. Chasidus was accused of attempting to supplant Torah learning as the *sine qua non* of Judaism. Memory of radical movements threatening the very existence of Judaism rendered any departure from the norm highly suspect. Not until the time of the Alter Rebbe, Rabbi Schneur Zalman of Liadi, who synthesized Chasidic fervor and worship with Lithuanian rationality and learning, could the movement make any significant inroads in the camp of the *mitnagdim*, the opponents of Chasidus. The Alter Rebbe's intellectual school of Chasidus was called Chabad. "The Baal Shem Tov demonstrated that everyone *can* serve G-d; the Alter Rebbe taught *how* everyone can serve G-d," describes their relative contributions.

While the Chasidic movement suffered a terrible blow—as did all the Jewish people—during the Second World War, it has shown remarkable vitality and viability, striking firm and productive roots on every continent. Interest in it, then, is not historical alone or theoretical, but immediate to any serious student of Judaism.

Chasidus, including Chabad, has been the subject of a great many studies in several languages. However, few of the sources were ever translated into English, and for the formidable subject matter, coupled with the specific definitions and connotations of Chabad terminology deter many potential students from exploring this field of study.

The essay *Kuntres Torat HaChasidus* ("Pamphlet on the Teachings of Chasidus") selected here for translation, was written by the sixth Lubavitcher Rebbe, Rabbi Yosef Yitzchak Schneersohn, of sainted memory. In discussing the general nature and contribution of Chabad, it is introductory in character.

In addition to the text of the essay proper, there is an excerpt from a letter composed by the author of the present work that addresses itself briefly to the same theme as our essay. The footnotes were prepared by the present Lubavitcher Rebbe, Rabbi Menachem M. Schneerson, excepting brief references and sources. Explanatory footnotes by the translator have been so marked.

"Translator's Explanatory Notes" have been included to facilitate the study of the essay. It is suggested that the reader examine these Notes at the outset, and then refer to them as the need arises. The translator has also added a brief Glossary of Hebrew terms, though the use of Hebrew has been kept to a minimum. The order of succession, describing the leaders of Chasidus and Chabad in sequence should allay confusion arising from names recurring in different generations.

It is hoped that both scholar and layman will find material in the present work to enlighten and broaden their vision of Judaism and Torah.

Rabbi Zalman I. Posner
Nashville, Tennessee
Adar I, 5719
(February 1959)

AUTHOR'S PREFACE

IN ANSWER TO the question regarding the study of Chasidus and its character, and its effects in elevating man; the manner of "service of the heart," i.e. prayer,[1] and its effect in actualizing the wisdom of Chasidus in daily life; and the need for the two [Chasidus and prayer] in the total service of G-d, which is the mission of the Jewish people—I will reply point by point.

---

1. *Taanit* 2a.

CHAPTER ONE

Chasidus Chabad—
Comprehension and Inspiration

Three are bound together: Israel, Torah, and G-d, all on
different planes, one higher than the other, partly concealed
and partly revealed."[1] In all three—Israel, Torah, and G-d—
there are both hidden and revealed dimensions. The revealed
dimension of Torah, *mitzvot* [religious obligations], and
G-dliness, is expounded in the Talmud, the codes and the early
and later commentaries. The esoteric dimension of Torah,
mitzvot, and G-d is discussed in Midrashic literature, *Zohar* and
Kabbalah, religious philosophy, and *Musar* [ethical works].

"The Almighty uncovered His holy arm"[2] and enlightened
us through the Baal Shem Tov and his disciples, our holy
forebears, the exponents of Chasidus. Chasidus merges the
concealed and revealed into one whole. To a certain degree,
through its various interpretations Chasidus reveals the inner
dimension of the Torah and its commandments, and stimulates
a G-dly feeling in the living heart of the Jew.

Chabad Chasidus, especially, is a Divine philosophy that
opens the gateways of wisdom and understanding to knowledge
and intellectual recognition of "He Who spoke and the world
came into being."[3] It shows every individual, each according to

---

1. *Zohar* III, 73a.
2. [Allusion to Isaiah 52:10. Incorporating biblical and rabbinic expressions in
    Chasidic writings is a common practice.]
3. Prayer Book. Morning Service.

his capabilities, how to draw near to Holiness, and how to serve G-d with his heart and mind.

Though a profound and exacting doctrine, Chabad Chasidus fully explains the most subtle concepts with examples and illustrations that are easily grasped, making such concepts accessible and understandable even to the ordinary intellect. Like all disciplines, Chasidus progresses from the simple to the difficult, leading the student, rung by rung, up the ladder of wisdom and knowledge.

The true value and uniqueness of Chasidus, however, lie in its power to arouse in the heart the emotions consonant with the subjects studied.

CHAPTER TWO

The Spiritual Heights
Reached even by Common Folk
Part I

THE BAAL SHEM Tov opened the channel of divine service by showing how every Jew can serve Him with love and reverence. Even simple folk, through sincere recitation of prayers and Psalms (though possibly ignorant of the words' meaning) and through love of fellow Jews, achieve an inner closeness to G-d. For the overriding consideration is the actual deed, and sincerity in one's divine service.

In the time of the Baal Shem Tov, a community was threatened with severe Divine punishment. Aware of the frightful state of affairs, the Baal Shem Tov prayed unusually long that Rosh Hashana and Yom Kippur. During the *Ne'ila* prayers his students saw that something most serious was amiss, and they too prayed from the depth of their hearts, with tears and heartfelt supplication.

Witnessing the fervent, heartrending prayers of the Baal Shem Tov and his disciples, the men and women in the synagogue were moved to join them in tearful prayer.

It was time for *Maariv*—the Holy Day should have come to an end—and still the Baal Shem Tov and his disciples prayed with increased fervor. Obviously something extraordinarily grave was involved, and the entire congregation wept from the depths of their hearts, creating a great commotion in the synagogue.

For several years now a Jewish shepherd lad had been attending High Holy Day services in the prayer-house of the Baal Shem Tov. A total illiterate, he would simply stand there, listening attentively, and stare into the *chazan's* face. Not a word did he utter.

A country boy, he was expert in imitating the sounds of animals—goats, sheep, birds and fowl. His favorite was the crow of the rooster. Upon seeing the excitement in the synagogue now, and hearing the weeping and wailing of the worshippers, he could contain himself no longer, and loudly cried, "Cock-a-doodle-doo! G-d, have mercy!"

CHAPTER THREE

The Spiritual Heights
Reached even by Common Folk
Part II

WHEN THIS BIZARRE call was heard in the synagogue the men were startled and the women terrified. Where could this strange sound have come from? But when the lad shouted, "G-d, have mercy!" they saw who it was. Some of the people standing near him wanted to expel him from the synagogue. But he retorted, "I am also a Jew. Your G-d is my G-d, too."

The aged sexton, Reb Yosef Yuzpa, calmed the worshippers and told the villager to remain in his place. A few minutes after this incident the congregation heard the Baal Shem Tov and his disciples hurrying to conclude the service. The Master's face radiated with joy. With rare spirit and delight the Baal Shem Tov ended *Ne'ila*, and with deep emotion he recited the verses *Shema*, *Boruch Shem*, and *Hashem Hu HaElokim* that mark the close of the Yom Kippur services. Then he sang joyous melodies.

Later that evening, during the meal, the Baal Shem Tov described to his disciples the danger that had hovered over the unfortunate community. He found, when pleading mercy for the community in question, that he was himself under censure for advocating settlement of Jews in villages and rural areas where they might be adversely influenced by the non-Jewish environment.

"As the deeds and status of the Jewish villagers were being examined, I saw that the charges were substantial and I was dismayed. But suddenly the lad's voice was heard On High, calling, 'Cock-a-doodle-doo! G-d have mercy!' His simple but sincere prayer caused such Heavenly delight that all accusations against the community and myself were nullified."

TRANSLATOR'S NOTE: Despite superficial similarities, this story is fundamentally different from the many non-Jewish folk tales that have as their theme the virtue of simple faith. In this case the lad's cry was effective because it alone could refute the accusations.

The charges stressed the deterioration of the Jew in isolation from his fellows; the rebuttal could not come from the sublime prayers of the saint, the Baal Shem Tov, since he was certainly no example of the inviolability of the *simple* Jewish soul.

It had to come from one who ostensibly exemplified the negative effects of village life, the shepherd. The account demonstrates the integrity of the Jew's soul, since the boy's deep-rooted feelings were acceptable to G-d despite his ignorance.

CHAPTER FOUR

Chasidus Animates the Mind
Prayer Unites the Mind and Heart
in the Service of G-d

IN HIS CHASIDIC writings, the Alter Rebbe, Rabbi Schneur Zalman of Liadi, teaches how those attempting to draw closer to Holiness by serving G-d with mind and heart, and putting piety into practice—in our relation with our Creator through fulfillment of the *mitzvot*, as well as in our relationship with our fellows—can achieve this through logical comprehension of the Divine.

During one of the *farbrengens* [Chasidic gatherings] of the early Chasidim, marking the bar-mitzvah of Rabbi DovBer, the Alter Rebbe's son, the subject of discussion was the advent of *Mashiach* and the resurrection of the dead. One of the Chasidim declared that the Alter Rebbe "enlivens the dead." He explained that the dead are cold and insensitive; movement and feeling are indications of life. "Is there anything as cold and unexcitable as the brain?" he asked. "When the cold brain comprehends and is moved by a G-dly concept, isn't that a form of resurrection of the dead?"

Chasidus illuminates and vivifies everything. It opens our eyes enabling us to perceive within every creature—inanimate, vegetative, animal, or human—the word of G-d that gives it existence and life, as evidenced in a remark by the Alter Rebbe.

On the second evening of *Succot*, 5660 (1899), the fifth Lubavitcher Rebbe, Rabbi Shalom DovBer, related, "One hundred years have now passed since the conversation between the Alter Rebbe and his son Rabbi DovBer on the subject of prayer, as recounted by the *"Tzemach Tzedek,"* Rabbi Menachem Mendel, to his son Rabbi Shmuel, the third and fourth Rebbes. During the holiday repast on the second evening of *Succot,* 5560 (1799), the Alter Rebbe asked his son on what subject he had meditated during the prayers of the past Rosh Hashana. Rabbi DovBer replied, 'I prayed with meditation on, *The lofty shall bow before You.'* [1] He then proceeded to ask the Alter Rebbe: 'And you, with what meditation did you pray?'

"The Alter Rebbe answered, 'I prayed with the *stender*—the wooden prayer book stand, while meditating on the fact that the existence of physical matter derives from His Essence.'"

Prayer, then, is the medium for fusing intellectual concepts with the emotions of the heart, and translating both into the practical fulfillment of *mitzvot* and the perfection of finer moral qualities.

---

1. Shabbat morning prayer.

CHAPTER FIVE

The First Step in the Elucidation of a Subject is to Analyze the Effects of its Study

IN EXPLICATING ANY subject, the interpretation must bear close relationship with the subject. Regardless of the effort expended in clarifying the subject with intelligible examples and parallels drawn from daily living, and presenting them lucidly, one cannot, and must not, create a barrier between the subject matter and its elucidation. Relevance of subject and illustration is indispensable, and only then is the explanation valid.

For example, the terms used by a carpenter or tailor in describing the qualities of their products must differ from those employed by a musician in interpreting his art; interpretations concerning astronomy will differ from those concerning medicine. Likewise, psychological explanations must differ in approach from those employed in theology. Each field has its individual style and fundamental premise.

Though Chabad Chasidus is intrinsically a profound and penetrating theology, the techniques involved in its study are the same as those employed in other profound studies.

The basic premise of Chasidus is that man's mission and the purpose of the soul's descent into the body, is the attainment of perfection in Divine service, in love and awe of G-d, and through proper conduct in social intercourse. These goals are to be achieved through meditation on and understanding of "How abundant are Your works"[1] and "How great are Your works."[2] All this is well within the capabilities of every Jew, but only through the study of Torah and the observance of its commandments.

Every concept or idea, be it ever so profound and abstract, must arouse an emotion consonant with that concept,[3] and find some practical expression in daily life.

The practical effect resulting from the emotion, which itself was generated by the idea, validates the veracity of the concept. Since human comprehension proceeds from the later state to the earlier one (from comprehension to concept,[4] development to nucleus, existence to character),[5] interpretation must therefore start with the effect. Then one may reasonably hope to comprehend the cause.

---

1. Psalms 104:24.
2. Ibid., 92:6.
3. [See Translator's Explanatory Notes on *Emotion Powers*.]
4. [Tr. Expl. Notes on *Intellect Powers*. Reference here is to exposition, not original thinking. Hence the developed idea precedes its nucleus.]
5. [One can be aware of the existence of some object yet ignorant of its nature, its character. Knowledge of *mehut*, of character, is the knowledge of what precisely that object is. Before analyzing the object one must know of its existence, hence the reference to *existence* and *character* as progressive stages.]

CHAPTER SIX

The Particulars of a Sacrificial Offering as Paralleled in Prayer

THE REBBE, RABBI Shalom DovBer begins his first treatise[1] written for the students of the Yeshiva Tomchei Tmimim,[2] with these words:

"Inasmuch as all the Chasidim inquire as to how one is to pray, and how one is to serve G-d through worship, I will explain this subject briefly."

Prayer is the foundation of Torah and *mitzvot* in their entirety. Hence, the first step in approaching the service of G-d must be through prayer. Our sages tell us that nowadays prayers take the place of the sacrificial offerings offered in the Sanctuary.[3] These offerings required several conditions: confession, placing one's hands on the offering, ritual slaughter, sprinkling its blood, and burning its fats. Above all, the following had to be clear: the identity of one bringing the offering; the significance of the offering; and to Whom it was being sacrificed.

In prayer, too, these same conditions are found. The worshipper is the one bringing the "offering." The prayers themselves include many analogies to the sacrifices. A sacrifice

---

1. *Kuntres HaTefillah* (*Tract on Prayer*). Written in 1900, fifth edition printed in Brooklyn, 1946. [English rendition, Brooklyn, 1992.]
2. [Talmudical and Rabbinical academy founded by Rabbi Sholom DovBer in 1897 in Lubavitch, now a network of such schools on every continent.]
3. *Brachot* 26b.

symbolized the subjugation of the person's natural traits and habits. Sometimes prayers contain a confession and other aspects of the offering. Primarily, prayer addresses the fulfillment of a need. One must realize, then, that one lacks something, and what, quantitatively and qualitatively, it is that one lacks. A petition for a trivial need cannot be compared to the depth and feeling of a supplication for a need that touches one's soul.

Similarly, one must be cognizant of the authority and stature of the person to whom the plea is directed. Making a request of a minor official is quite different than pleading before one vested with power over life and death. Therefore, a person must know the scope of authority and the degree of power wielded by the one to whom the petition is addressed.

Divine judgment and anger are different from their counterparts in mortals. In the Talmud[4] we find the following account:

> When Rabbi Yochanan ben Zakai became ill, his students visited him. Seeing them, he wept. They exclaimed, 'Light of Israel! Pillar of strength! Mighty Hammer! Why do you weep?' Replied the Sage, 'Were I being led before a mortal king, who is here today and in the grave tomorrow; who, if he should be angry with me, his anger is not eternal, and if he should imprison me, the imprisonment is not everlasting, and if he should kill me, it is not for eternity; whom I can appease with words or bribe with money— nonetheless I would weep. Now that I am being led before the King of Kings, the Eternal, Whose anger is eternal,

---

4. *Brachot* 28b.

Who can imprison me for eternity, Who can decree eternal death for me, Whom I can neither placate with words nor bribe with money....'

Though prayer is the expression of the heart's innermost depths, it must satisfy certain conditions: self-appraisal i.e., awareness of the petitioner's own character, is he worthy enough? if not, is he improving himself to attain worthiness?; understanding of the importance of prayer, and meditation on Him to Whom one is praying.

Chapter Seven

Man—The Core of Creation

In Hebrew, MAN has four distinct names: *adam*, *ish*, *enosh* and *gever*. Each of these terms describes a special virtue of man, and a failing.

Adam refers to a man of wisdom and understanding; *ish* is descriptive of moral, emotive attributes;[1] *enosh* signifies weakness in either intellect or emotions; *gever* denotes strength and mastery over obstacles, either in the realm of the intellect or of the emotions, whether or not the strength is innate or acquired.

Adam is the loftiest adjective, that of intellectual capacity. Through this trait a person, striving with mind and heart, achieves superiority over all Creation, not only over terrestrial creatures, but even over spiritual ones, such as the ministering angels and emanations.[2] Though the angels (on high) are Abstract Intellects[3] (despite their "bodily" existence)—since their conceptions are non-spatial and non-temporal, while those of humans are circumscribed by the limitations of time and space—still man is superior. For only man has been given the mission and ability to illumine the darkness of this physical world with the light of Torah and *mitzvot*, to make it a G-dly

---

1. [Tr. Expl. Notes on *Emotion Powers*.]
2. [Tr. Expl. Notes on *Four Worlds*.]
3. [Angels do not, of course, exist in physical form, but as intellectual beings. Their *bodies* are the forms intellect may assume, with the concomitant limitations of intellect.]

abode.[4] The Abstract Intellects lack this ability. Moreover, they cannot even conceive that physical objects can serve as an "abode" for the Divine Majesty, or that a physical brain can conceive of G-d.

Man alone was chosen by G-d for this task. Therefore he is called the "principal creature." He has no parallel among the higher or lower creatures. Indeed, since he is composed of the loftiest and the lowest components (his body being formed from the lowest gross matter—dust of the earth, and his soul from the highest of all—"part of G-d above")[5] man with his physical brain can grasp G-dly concepts even more thoroughly than can the angels.[6] This dual composition of man, makes him superior to the heavenly creatures.

––––––––––––––––––––

4. [Tr. Expl. Notes on *Tetragrammaton* and *Condensation*. Through performance of His will as expressed in the Torah, the physical objects used and the person performing become vessels for the Divine. They provide a dwelling-place for Him in the physical world where His presence is not obvious. The expression regarding G-d's "desiring an abode among the lower" worlds and creatures is found in *Tanchuma, Noso*, 16.]

5. Job, 31:2. See *Tanya*, beginning of ch. 2.

6. [Man alone has unlimited capacity for spiritual advancement. Other creatures, including angels, have an ordained status they cannot transcend.]

CHAPTER EIGHT

A Narrative about the Maggid
His Lesson on Man's Virtue – Part One

THE ALTER REBBE once told his brother, Rabbi Yehuda Leib (author of *She'erit Yehuda*), about his first visit to his teacher, Rabbi DovBer, the Maggid of Mezritch. Rabbi Yehuda Leib later related the account to Rabbi Menachem Mendel, third Rebbe of Lubavitch.

Once the members of the Chasidic fraternity[1] were discussing the various levels of angels associated with the Divine Chariot and the counterparts of these angels in every world.[2] One of the disciples spoke of the angels as Abstract Intellects whose very life is the Word of G-d.[3] Another spoke of those celestial beings as continually in alternating states of Love and Fear, of "advance and retreat";[4] another, of still loftier

---

1. [Lit. "members of the Holy Society." These were the disciples of Rabbi DovBer, Maggid of Mezritch, successor to the Baal Shem Tov, founder of the Chasidic movement. After the Maggid's demise, the disciples assumed leadership of the Chasidim in their respective communities.]
2. [Tr. Expl. Notes on *Four Worlds*. Beings of a higher world are paralleled on lower planes by correspondingly lower yet analogous beings. The terms used in Ezekiel 1:10, for example, may be applied to physical creatures or to their counterparts in higher, non-corporeal worlds.]
3. [Rabbi Schneur Zalman's *Shaar Hayichud V'ha'emuna*, ch. 1. The Word of G-d "let there be..." (Gen. 1) brought Creation into being *ex nihilo* (Tr. Expl. Notes on *Thought and Speech*). With a retraction of the Word, all existence would revert to its previous, non-existent state. Hence the life-force is His vivifying Word. In this physical world, this is not perceived by the senses; in the spiritual worlds the Word is consciously felt.]
4. See Rashi's commentary on Ezekiel 1:4.

beings. Several of the disciples discussed the *sefirot*[5] of *Atzilut*, elaborating on the superiority of *tiferet* over the other attributes, the superiority of *bina* over the emotive-attributes, and the superiority of *chochma* over *bina*, etc. All these have this in common: they are intellectual emanations possessing knowledge and understanding, each praising and glorifying its Creator in its own way.

The impassioned discussion of the wondrously sweet service of the heavenly beings, and envious of that exalted level, kindled a fire of longing for G-d in the hearts of all the disciples. They were overwhelmed by a state of ecstasy. Moving their lips silently, they trembled and wept. Some stood with faces flushed, eyes shining, and hands outstretched, as though thunder-struck. Others among them sang quietly, their hearts bursting, and their souls on the verge of expiration in intense yearning to cleave to their Maker.

"My brother told me," related Rabbi Yehuda Leib, "that this scene clarified for him the words of Rabbi Shimon bar Yochai, 'I bound myself with a single bond, I became one with Him; I was aflame with Him.'

"No doubt," continued my brother, "had the Maggid not entered the hall at that moment, some of the men would have simply expired as a result of their tremendous yearning and desire to unite with the Almighty. But as soon as the Maggid's footsteps were heard, the entire group instantly came out of their reverie and prepared themselves to receive their mentor.

---

5. [Tr. Expl. Notes for discussion of all these terms.]

CHAPTER NINE

A Narrative about the Maggid
His Lesson on Man's Virtue – Part Two

"THE MAGGID TOOK his usual seat at the head of the table and began:

"I made the earth, and Man thereon I created."[1] *Anochi* [Hebrew for "I"], He Who is the true *I*, unknown to and concealed from even the loftiest emanations, clothed His Essence through numerous condensations to give rise to emanations and creatures, the various categories of angels, and worlds without number. Through countless contractions 'I made this physical world and thereon created Man.' Man is the ultimate purpose of Creation. *Barati* [Hebrew for 'I have created'], the numerical equivalent[2] of 613 [the number of Biblical commandments], is the *raison d'être* of Man. As [the book of] *Pardes* (Portal 22, ch. 4) quotes *Sefer HaBahir*, 'Said the attribute of *Chesed* [Kindness] before the Holy One, 'Master of the Universe, since the days of Avraham I have had no work to do, because Avraham serves in my stead.' For Avraham, a soul clothed in a body, occupying himself with hospitality to strangers as a means of promulgating the idea of G-d, is thus higher than the attribute of *Chesed* itself in its most sublime state in *Atzilut*. The 'complaint' of *Chesed*—is the expression of envy of *Chesed* of *Atzilut* of the service of our Patriarch Abraham."

---

1. Isaiah 45:12.
2. [Hebrew letters have numerical value (e.g. *aleph* is 1, *bet* is 2, etc.).]

Concluding his words, the Maggid retired to his quarters. His brief discourse had a calming, reviving effect on his disciples.

"I witnessed two things then," remarked the Alter Rebbe, "The holy ecstasy of the Chasidic fraternity, and the remarkable composure of the Maggid, which captivated my entire being. It was then that I became a Chasid."

On Monday, *Elul* 13, 5652 (1892), during the wedding celebration of my uncle Rabbi Moshe HaCohen[3], my father, of sainted memory, retold this story and explained:

> "The [Alter] Rebbe, the Lithuanian genius, Talmudist, philosopher and Kabbalist, became a Chasid not because of the ecstasy over heavenly angels, but because of the intellectual composure of the Maggid of Mezritch.

The Rebbe assimilated the profound concept that the highest attribute of *Chesed* envies a man who acts hospitably for G-d's sake. To the principle that every Jew must serve G-d with his maximum of understanding, the Alter Rebbe devoted his life."

---

3. Horenstein.

CHAPTER TEN

Revelation of this Virtue: Only Through Toil

THE MAGGID'S LESSON teaches us the wondrous distinction of man and his intellectual and moral attributes. Through the subjugation of his intellect to the service of G-d, he is more exalted than the highest of the high. Now all this concerns man as he was created; he is endowed at the outset with the potentialities of the ideal man, to fulfill his mission in life, the goal of the soul's descent into the physical world. It must be understood that these are only potential. To realize these potentialities entails strenuous effort.

By way of illustration: when one desires to build a house, it is not enough to have the land and materials required for the construction; they do not become a house by themselves. Someone must expend effort to transform the materials into a building, and the effort is considerable.

There is a difference, however, between the illustration and our subject. Materials and craftsmanship, coupled with considerable effort, are all that is needed in the construction of a physical edifice. Not so in the "building" of a man in achieving self-fulfillment. For although G-d grants man the materials and potentialities required for the task, yet another factor must be considered—the materials, so to speak, are mixed up, and clothed in soiled garments.

In the earth, the most brilliant diamond is found encrusted in impurities. The gem must first be mined and then properly cleansed in order to reveal its G-d given brilliance. Man, the diamond shining with the "light that is good,"[1] is born clothed in gross garments, with impurities of mind and heart that must, as in the case of the diamond, be removed. Then, his soul will shine within him and he will fulfill his Divinely ordained mission in life.

---

1. [Allusion to Gen. 1:4. See fn. 1.]

CHAPTER ELEVEN

Three Types of Endeavor

THIS SERVICE—ATTAINING the predominance of form over matter,[1] leading away from the material towards the spiritual—is difficult indeed. It is a three-fold task for which great skill is necessary: 1) breaking away from the material, 2) coming closer to the spiritual, and 3) effecting the superiority of form over matter. It involves three ascending types of endeavor: 1) subjugation and rejection of matter, 2) cognizance of the virtue of the spiritual, and an inclination toward it, and 3) mastery of form over matter.

These three types of endeavor correspond with three disciplines: 1) concentrating on the subjugation of matter and exposing its unworthiness; 2) recognition of the qualities of the spiritual, and understanding that the spiritual is the basis of all physical existence; and 3) cultivation of the mastery of form over matter, which in turn is sub-divided into two categories: a) sublimation and purification of matter to render it compatible with form, and b) emphasis on the quality of form as embodied in matter.

These three schools are hallowed philosophies that lead to the recognition of the Creator and His service through Torah study and the fulfillment of His *mitzvot*. Nevertheless, they are distinct schools and stand on different levels. Each is a rung in the soul-ladder "standing on earth whose top reaches Heaven."[2]

---

1. [Tr. Expl. Notes.]
2. Gen. 28:12.

CHAPTER TWELVE

Musar, Chakira and Chasidus

THE FIRST OF these schools is predicated on the subjugation of the material and demonstrating its unworthy crassness. This includes any improper propensities one might possess, such as overindulging in eating and other physical delights in common with animals. When a human conducts himself like an animal, he debases himself even more than a brute creature. For lacking the power of reason, an animal is unable to desire anything loftier than its own physical gratification. A human, however, is endowed with intelligence enabling him to aspire to something higher, to moral virtue, to intellectual values. When he prefers physical pleasures he is more degenerate than an animal. This school, which rejects the material by depicting the baseness of physical pleasures and passions, and by describing their dire consequences, is the school of *Musar*.

The second school stresses the qualities of the spiritual, of morality and intellect. It teaches the means of attaining these higher goals, exalting them as the basis of perfection and the aim of Creation, making this world a fitting fulfillment of His "desire for an abode in the lower"[1] worlds. This is the school of *Chakira*, religious philosophy.

The highest school expounds the superiority of form over matter. It emphasizes the value of purified matter (physical matter that is consecrated to a higher, spiritual purpose, and that thus ceases to be "merely" physical); and of form when embodied in matter (the spiritual that influences and elevates

---

1. Tr. Expl. Notes on *Four Worlds*.

physical matter, and itself is no longer "merely" ethereal), in an inseparable and harmonious union. In this union there is no beginning or ending, no superior or inferior; each is essential to the other; each is implanted within the other. One G-d created them both for the identical purpose of revealing His Holy Light, and only in perfect unity do they achieve the perfection He desired. This is the approach of Chasidus.

CHAPTER THIRTEEN

Faith and Knowledge

THE THREE SCHOOLS—*Musar, Chakira* and Chasidus—are mutually dependent. The first is a basis and step toward the second; the second complements the first and becomes the basis and step toward the third. The third completes the other two in that it brings into rational perspective the basic principle of creation: "The foundation of foundations and pillar of wisdoms, [is] to know that there is a First Existence Who brings into being every existence, and all that exist in heaven and earth and between them, exist only by virtue of His existence" (Maimonides[1]).

This singular expression of Maimonides,[2] "*to know* that there is a First Existence" rather than *to believe*, has frequently been discussed. It indicates the obligation to understand this subject to the best of one's abilities. Maimonides goes even further, saying,[3] "The knowledge of this principle is a positive commandment, included in the first words of the Ten Commandments—*I am the L-rd your G-d.*" Now the words[4] "I

---

1. *Yad Hachazaka, Hilchot Yesodai HaTorah,* beginning.
2. Maimonides in *Sefer Hamitzvot* (Positive Commandment, 1) says, "that we believe." However, 1) the *Yad* is a later work than *Sefer Hamitzvot* which is introductory (cf. Introduction, *Yad*); 2) the text of *Sefer Hamitzvot* is not as precise (cf. *Yad Malachi, Klalai HaRambam,* 23; 3) *Sefer Hamitzvot* is a translation, hence an error may have occurred (ibid. 22), while the *Yad* was written in Hebrew; 4) some Arabic ms. permit the translation to read "to know." Cf. *Minyan Hamitzvot,* beginning of *Yad*; *Sefer Hamitzvot,* ed. Heller. (Footnote by Rabbi Menachem M. Schneerson, the Lubavitcher Rebbe.)
3. *Yad,* "Yesodai HaTorah," Law 6.
4. Ex. 20:2.

am . . . ," contain the obligation of faith, yet even here Maimonides employs the term knowledge.

The connection here between faith and knowledge is this: The duty of faith concerns pure, simple faith, transcending the realm of intellect. But first one must strive with one's mind to grasp to the extent of one's intellectual capacities. Beyond that limit of understanding, he is to believe with simple faith.[5] By achieving the maximum of understanding, and by following it with faith, one fulfills the *mitzvah* of faith to perfection. For his faith is pure, encompassing nothing that might be understood.

---

5. *Yad*, ibid.

CHAPTER FOURTEEN

The Parameters of Wisdom

IT IS OBVIOUS that every field of study has its own framework and parameters. Though all branches of knowledge share common principles, they are not equally applicable to all sciences. Natural science can never be quite equal to the metaphysical science of the soul, let alone to Torah and the study of the Creator.

When we speak of features common to all sciences or wisdoms, we refer to an attribute such as enlightenment, for example. But the enlightenment obtained from the study of nature is, of course, not comparable to the enlightenment achieved through Torah study.

As in all wisdoms, the three schools of thought discussed above, though complementary and interdependent, have each their unique terms of reference that indicate their particular essential qualities. Moreover, since the three schools stand in ascending order, it follows that their essential qualities follow in the same order.

CHAPTER FIFTEEN

The Objective of Wisdom—Concrete Action

THE QUALITIES OF the respective wisdoms that give one superiority over the other and contrast them—are basically spiritual elements. Still they manifest their differences also in their application and in the limitations of their resultant actions. For example, the powers of the soul, though spiritual, are particular powers delimited by their actions through the physical body. The intellectual powers of the soul (Concept, Comprehension, and Concentration)[1] are, of course, spiritual. Still they use distinct compartments of the physical brain. Each has its unique quality—the creativeness of Concept, the grasp of Comprehension, and the depth of Concentration. The same is true of all wisdoms: though spiritual, they are fulfilled through their action and influence on the physical and material, in which their purpose and truth are manifested.

The terms "purpose" and "truth" are used advisedly, being two essentials of the very existence of all creatures. G-d has created every single one of His creatures with a specific purpose in mind. Fulfillment of its purpose, and achievement of its goal, renders its existence true and complete.

Because the ultimate expression of every wisdom is its translation into action in the physical sense, there is a corresponding physical body suitable to every wisdom, capable of bringing that wisdom into fruition. The Creator endowed each wisdom with the power to overcome every opposition or

---

1. [Tr. Expl. Notes on *Intellect Powers*.]

hindrance, and to realize its purpose, from potentiality to actual deed. The deed, the results, then verify and fulfill that wisdom.

There is an expression, "None is as wise as the experienced."[2] "Wise" refers to one endowed with wisdom, just as "seer" would apply to one endowed with sight. The description "seer" is applicable only when the power of sight is exercised; one sitting in darkness cannot very well be called a seer. Similarly, "Wise" is descriptive of wisdom in action and realization, or, as in the above expression, in experience.

---

2. *Akedas Yitzchak*, XIV.

CHAPTER SIXTEEN

The Product Corresponds to the Wisdom

THE ACTION OR result of each wisdom must conform with the basic character of that wisdom. In any particular thought, the result or decision will conform to the creativity, comprehension and profundity exercised therein. In every type of wisdom and science likewise, the results will be determined by the character of that science. In the practical sciences, the effectiveness of a machine produced by the exercise of skill and mastery of a particular science, will verify that science's validity. Every wisdom will be substantiated and fulfilled by its particular results inasmuch as the consummate expression of every wisdom is in action. Since the results validate the wisdoms, the qualities and relative standing of such results will vary in accordance with their respective wisdoms in degree and sequence.

Now let us examine the practical effects of the three schools discussed above. In the case of the *Musar* school, the aim is the rejection and negation of the material. The practical effect is the repudiation of unseemly moral traits and the acquisition of the finer ones.

The aim of *Chakira*, religious philosophy, is the recognition of the virtue of intellectual pursuits, particularly of Torah. Its practical effect is occupation with study, and withdrawal from mundane affairs.

The aim of the third school is the recognition of the essential qualities of form and substance. It leads to the dominance of form to the extent that substance itself becomes form, viz., physical matter becomes a vehicle for G-dliness.

CHAPTER SEVENTEEN

Force, Light, Vitality

EACH OF THE three schools of thought has its specific axis, the pivot around which it revolves. These are described in Chasidus respectively as *force*, *light* and *vitality*.

The fundamental principle of *Musar*, its nucleus and pivotal premise, is *force*—the decisive repudiation and abhorrence of the undesirable physical attributes of matter, stressing the unreality of the material.

The foundation of *Chakira* is the illuminating *light*—extolling intellectual activity, and recognizing the spiritual intellect alone as the basis of everything.

The basis of Chasidus, its nucleus and pivot, is the *vitality* that vivifies even the lowest material being. It demonstrates the ultimate reason for the creation of gross matter, namely, that it be transformed into form. Chasidus endows even gross matter with spiritual life.

CHAPTER EIGHTEEN

Musar and *Chakira* in Chasidus and their Virtue

THOUGH CHARACTERISTICALLY DISTINCT, these three nuclei have a definite relationship, wherein the higher includes within itself the lower. In the relation of Force to Light, Light includes Force, and both are in turn included within Vitality. It must be understood that Force and Light, as they are included in Vitality, do not retain their original characters, as when they exist independently. In its inclusion within Light, Force assumes Light-qualities; and both Force and Light when included in Vitality, acquire Life-qualities.

Hence, in the three schools the respective qualities, their nuclei, of Force, Light and Vitality, are qualitatively higher when they appear in subordinate states, i.e., as part of the higher nucleus, than they are when they appear in their independent, pristine states. In other words, *Musar* as a consequence of *Chakira*, and both *Musar* and *Chakira* as consequences of Chasidus, are radically different from *Musar* and *Chakira per se.*

A higher wisdom can be attained only by progressive ascent from the lower stages. In our case, one must begin with *Musar*-of-Chasidus, or the Light element of Vitality. Finally one reaches Vitality itself, the essence of Chasidus.

CHAPTER NINETEEN

The Greater the Person, the Greater his Evil Inclination

"HE WHO STARVES himself is sated; he who satisfies himself is starved," is a principle concerning physical pleasures. Our sages tell us,[1] "The greater the person, the greater his Evil Impulse." The cause of this greater Evil Inclination is the person himself.[2] Since he considers himself "great," he uses his Torah knowledge to rationalize his self-gratification. This results in an increased propensity toward Evil.

Before beginning to study Chasidus, a person may be gross to a degree unbefitting his scholarship and piety. For "man is born a wild colt,"[3] following his natural traits, adoring himself and taking pride in his virtues. Thus one may conduct himself according to the dictates of the Torah, violating no prohibitions and fulfilling the positive duties as required, yet, as Nachmanides observes in his commentary,[4] "one can be abominable within the strict framework of the Torah."

It is distressing that so many pious and learned people who behave according to Torah law, often employ so many devious arguments to justify themselves. They exploit their scholarship

---

1. *Succah* 52a.

2. [The word *mimenu* – "ממנו" כל הגדול מחבירו יצרו גדול "ממנו" – meaning *than his*, may be rendered *from himself*.]

3. Job 11:12.

4 Commentary on Torah, beginning of *Kedoshim*.

possess fine characters, who conduct themselves according to the exhortations of *Musar*, but who are nonetheless brutish and deluded in their self-appraisal. One meets pious people, who are punctilious in religious observance, possessing of fine traits of character, yet are small-minded and complacent with their level of attainment.

Even intellectuals and scholars, devotees of the school of *Chakira*, are for the most part arrogant and self-styled sages whose character traits are not the most admirable. The more they advance intellectually, the more their arrogance grows.

The reason for this is that "sin lies at the door,"[6] and, "The imagination of man's heart is evil from his youth."[7] The Evil Impulse enters man at birth, takes root, and grows through indulgence in desires and passions for food and drink and other physical needs. To be sure, whatever he does is permitted by the Torah—he eats and drinks only permitted foods, but he is drawn to them, desires them and derives pleasure from them.

---

6. Gen. 4:7.
7. Gen. 8:21.

CHAPTER TWENTY

Self-Delusion

THE FOOL WALKS in darkness."[1] Since he walks in darkness he deems the bitter to be sweet.

The Evil Impulse is called a craftsman: "This is the craft of the *yetzer hara*, the Evil Impulse: today it says, *Do this*; tomorrow it says, *Do that*; finally it says, *Go, worship idols*."[2] The Evil Impulse's skill lies in its ability to adapt itself to the individual's situation. It appeals to people of stature in their terms, and to the lowly in theirs, rationalizing indulgence in pleasure, arguing its necessity in maintaining physical health, or insisting on attire and a home commensurate with the individual's supposed prestige.

Above all, this *yetzer hara* gives the individual an exaggerated estimation of his stature, his intellectual capacities, his morality and personal conduct. Our Sages tell us,[3] "A man can see all afflictions except his own." Man is oblivious to his own shortcomings; he fails to recognize his personal faults. It happens so often that people who themselves are prey to undesirable moral traits, such as deceit and arrogance, will deprecate their fellows as liars and conceited individuals. These people are not only unaware of their own failings, ignorant of their pride and falseness, they vindicate their actions with all sorts of tortuous reasons.

---

1. Eccl.2:14.
2. *Shabbat* 105b.
3. *Negaim* II, 5.

CHAPTER TWENTY-ONE

The Unnoticed Malady of Self-Love

THE TURBID WELL-SPRING and corrupt source"[1] is the disease of self-love. Those afflicted with it are blinded, incapable of seeing the undeniable truth of their desperate situation; they lose sight of the correct path. Just as one who is physically ill may find food and drink a source of pain, the same is true with the spiritually ill, those who by nature are proud. The more knowledge of Torah they amass and the further they progress in *mitzvah* observance, the more important they consider themselves and the more arrogant they become.

Every disease has its malignant source, its core that gives it the power to grow and spread, and to wreak havoc on the body of the patient. The germ of the soul-sickness we described is ignorance of the illness. The person who knows that he is sick will seek means to be cured; he will expend all his resources to regain his health. If he lacks the means, then he will seek assistance from others sympathetic to his plight. But one who is unaware of his illness will not seek a cure, and will ultimately succumb.

---

1. [Allusion to Prov. 25:26.]

CHAPTER TWENTY-TWO

The Rebbe, Rabbi Shmuel, on Self-Delusion

THE WINTER OF 5642 (1882) was a period of unrest and trouble for Russian Jewry. My grandfather, the Rebbe, Rabbi Shmuel, spent an extended time in S. Petersburg on communal affairs, and called a number of meetings of leading Jewish figures. At one of these gatherings someone asked him what the Alter Rebbe had contributed with the founding of the Chasidic movement.

Rabbi Shmuel answered, "With the founding of the Chasidic movement, the Alter Rebbe contributed the principle that man know his shortcomings, and that deficiency is a disease."

The man who realizes that he is ill will seek a remedy, and the Healer of the sick will send him his cure. Not so in the case of an individual who supposes himself healthy. It is said that Mashiach will heal all the afflicted, except the fool, because the fool doesn't even know he is sick. A fool is not merely unaware of his foolishness; he considers himself wise. He fails to perceive any "light that is good."[1] He considers darkness to be light.

---

1. [Allusion to Gen. 1:4.]

CHAPTER TWENTY-THREE

The Necessity for Expunging the Filth of Self-Love

WHEN G-D GRANTS man the spirit to penetrate his blindness and open his mind's eye to recognize the evil in which he is immersed; when his heart is inspired to abandon the gross and despicable darkness, to proceed in the Light of Life along the path leading to the House of G-d, to know the Creator and be illumined with His Light—then first he must cleanse himself of all impurities of self-adulation. He must purify the soul's "garments" (thought, speech and deed)[1] and through self-discipline rigorously control his thinking, speech and actions. Evil or lustful thoughts, forbidden speech like slander or falsehood, and certainly sinful actions must become repugnant, and vigorously eliminated.

This is the service of one whom G-d inspired to escape from darkness, whose eyes were opened to perceive the light of Chasidus, and who thus literally becomes a new being. For, in truth, he has relinquished the darkness of error and brutishness for the light of Truth and Life. He must set a fixed period of time for self-examination in regard to all his past, namely, all of his delusions, concerning both his character traits and his conduct.

---

1. [Tr. Expl. Notes.]

CHAPTER TWENTY-FOUR

The First Step in Divine Service

MANY ERRONEOUSLY ASSUME that since they are desirous of approaching G-d through Chasidus, and have committed no definite transgressions, hence, by accepting and following Chasidic practices, they have already penetrated the inner sanctum of Holiness. This is a total, most serious mistake. True, "יפה שעה אחת בתשובה ומעשים טובים, one hour–שעה of repentance and good deeds is . . . desirable . . . ."[1] The meaning of *sha'ah* (שעה) is also "turn," as we find in *Rashi*'s comment on *lo sha'ah* (לא שעה) in Genesis 4:5. Through repentance and good deeds with but "one turn" a person is out of the darkness. Still, he is not yet cleansed of previously acquired impurities.

Hence, at the outset one must cleanse his intellect, emotions and soul-garbs, bathing himself with "hot" and "cold" water—the tears of a repentant heart, and the perspiration of exertion in the performance of *mitzvot*. Tears and perspiration have common physical qualities, and both may be either "hot" or "cold," but they differ in purpose and effect. This is discussed at length in Chasidic literature.

---

1. *Avot* 4:17.

CHAPTER TWENTY-FIVE

The Rebbe, Rabbi DovBer on
Circumcision Unfinished: Coarse Spirituality

THE MITTELER REBBE, Rabbi DovBer, while a child, studied the *Mishna*,[1] "Circumcision without severance of the membrane is not circumcision." He interpreted the *Mishna* in terms of man's service, in this manner: "He who performs on himself the *mitzvah* of circumcision, *You shall circumcise the obduracy of your hearts*,[2] beginning to serve G-d with love and awe, but has still not severed himself from his complete past, i.e., he does not strenuously fulfill, *Turn away from evil and do good*,[3] and yet considers himself *circumcised* and fit to progress in His service—such a person is not deemed *circumcised* at all."

Abandonment of darkness does not imply purification from his brutishness. As we have said about the haughty person, his very spiritual affairs are of a gross nature. Though he studies Torah and fulfills his religious obligations meticulously, and this is certainly "spiritual," but the spiritual itself is gross, because of his innate crassness. This is not to say that he is "not good" according to Torah standards; he may well be "good," but he is material and brutish nonetheless.

Until one has purified his intellect, emotions, and soul-garbs, he still stands on the outside, so to speak. Despite his divine service, his study of Chasidus or Torah in general, his

---

1. *Shabbat* 19: 6.
2. Deut. 10:16.
3. Psalms 34:1.

74

competence in the subject matter of his studies, his familiarity with the varieties of "service of the heart," his meditations on the concepts he has studied in Chasidus to the degree that his mind is inspired by the excellence of that concept and his heart is moved by a feeling of closeness and love of G-d, or conversely, of awe and fear of G-d—despite all this, he remains on the perimeter until he purifies his mind, emotion, thought, speech and deed.

CHAPTER TWENTY-SIX

A Vessel Used in Fire–A Lesson by the Alter Rebbe

A STUDENT IN one of the Alter Rebbe's *chedorim*,[1] who was an exceptionally gifted and profound thinker, was originally among the opponents of Chasidus and a scholar of renown before he joined the movement. When he arrived in Liozna[2] he immersed himself in the study of Chasidus, and quickly amassed a tremendous knowledge. He habitually meditated for hours on end on some subject of Chasidus.

Parenthetically, it is related that once when he was in ill health, he intended to get a good night's sleep after the Fast of the Tenth of *Tevet*.[3] Before reciting the *Shema* at bedside, he washed his hands[4] and stood near the window as he began his prayer. He stood there meditating until dawn. . . .

A cousin of this disciple related that in his first audience with the Alter Rebbe, the young man had asked, "Rebbe, what do I lack?"

---

1. Upon founding the Chabad movement, the Alter Rebbe assembled a number of gifted young men, proficient Talmudists, among them renowned scholars. They were divided into "seminars," (*chedorim*) — *cheder* 1, 2, and 3. He personally instructed them in Chasidus.
2. [Liozna was the first center of the Chabad movement under the Alter Rebbe.]
3. [Marking the start of the Babylonian siege of Jerusalem which culminated in the destruction of the Temple.]
4. [The *Shema* is recited upon retiring and arising daily. (Cf. Deut. 6:7; Prayer Book.) Before praying, it is customary to wash the hands.]

The Alter Rebbe answered, "You lack nothing. You are pious and a scholar. But you must rid yourself of the *chametz*,[5] self-awareness, and arrogance. You must instill within yourself *matzah*, renunciation of self. By law, a vessel used for *chametz* with fire can be made kosher for Passover use only by being subjected to heat intense enough to make sparks fly, or until the outer shell is removed."

Upon leaving the Rebbe's room the disciple remarked, "The Rebbe taught me a Passover law[6] as it is taught in *Gan Eden* (Paradise).[7] A vessel used with fire—a person so arrogant as to consider himself 'Light'[8] itself, thereby repelling the Divine Presence—must be purified through fire, through such intense white heat that sparks fly. That is the sparks of G-dliness within him and in the world around him, become elevated and united with the True Light. Thus the outer shell is removed. With this the Rebbe endowed me with the strength to fulfill in my divine service, the law of purification by fire. Thank G-d, I will concentrate on this objective in my prayers, and I hope to G-d that good results will follow."

---

5. [*Chametz* is the leaven that makes dough rise. It is symbolic of self-esteem, haughtiness. *Matzah* is the *bread of affliction, of poverty* (Passover Haggadah) that does not contain leavening, and does not rise. It is symbolic of humility. Jews are forbidden to eat *chametz* during Passover.]

6. *Shulchan Aruch Orach Chaim* 451, 4.

7. [I.e. according to the esoteric part of the Torah. See above p. 15ff.]

8. [In the original: אור *ohr*, the term used in the statement "a vessel used in fire." *Ohr* can mean both *fire* and *light*.]

CHAPTER TWENTY-SEVEN

Prayer: A Receptacle to the Light of Divine Service

PRAYER IS THE vessel for the Light that irradiates from practical Divine service, in the same way that the brain is the instrument for intellect and the heart for emotion. This means that in order for any concept, comprehension, or emotional inspiration to illumine one's daily life—by way of proper conduct and fine moral attributes—prayer is the indispensable prerequisite.

Since prayer is the vehicle for serving G-d in deed, it follows that prayer includes various categories and entails differing methods. For this reason prayer is described by different terms, such as "offering," "ladder," etc. All these terms, in their original Hebrew, describe prayer as an approach to G-d and a union with Him. This union itself has various stages.

The daily prayers vary according to the day itself. There are different prayers for weekdays, Shabbat, *Rosh Chodesh*, Festivals, High Holy Days, days commemorating miracles, etc. Each of these prayers is in a category of its own. Just as prayers vary with the occasion, so do they vary with the individual worshipper. Though the prayer text for any given day is the same for everyone, the mode of prayer and intensity of devotion will vary with the individual.

Despite all the variations, however, prayer is indispensable and basic to all religious activity and Divine service.

CHAPTER TWENTY-EIGHT

Teshuva and the *Avoda* of *Teshuva*:
An explanation by the Rebbe, Rabbi Shmuel

IN 5639 (1878), on the first Shabbat of Chanukah, my grandfather, Rabbi Shmuel, delivered the discourse beginning with the quotation,[1] "Serve G-d with joy." The basis of that discourse concerned the elucidation and interpretation of the degrees of joyous service. Among other things, Rabbi Shmuel declared that even repentance must be joyous, to say nothing of the service of repentance which must certainly be with joy.

My father, Rabbi Shalom DovBer, an exacting and precise student of his father's teachings, took note of this. He interpreted to himself the terms "repentance" and "service of repentance." The first relates primarily to those matters that must be completely rejected, for even the faintest trace of evil is evil, to be repelled. Though repentance of this sort entails tears of anguish for possessing evil, nonetheless, Rabbi Shmuel emphasized, even such repentance must be accompanied by joy, the joy of ridding oneself of evil. My father understood the term "service of repentance" to mean gradual progression to ever higher spiritual stages.

His interpretation not withstanding, my father decided to ask his father, Rabbi Shmuel, for clarification of the subject. Early Tuesday morning, the fourth day of Chanukah, he entered his father room and asked him to explain the difference between the terms used. Rabbi Shmuel explained, "*Repentance* is the practical act. *Service of repentance* refers to those things which engender practical actions. The quality of repentance

---

1. Psalms 100:2.

79

hinges on the nature of those things which give rise to it. Both come through prayer, the vehicle of practical service."

CHAPTER TWENTY-NINE

A Torah Lesson of the Alter Rebbe, the Maggid and R. Zusya of Anipoli

RABBI SHMUEL CONTINUED. "My father [Rabbi Menachem Mendel] repeated for me what the Alter Rebbe had told him during an audience on *Elul* 6, 5564 (1804). The previous Friday evening (*parshat Shoftim*)[1] an hour after lighting the Shabbat candles, the Alter Rebbe delivered the discourse on the verse, "Judges and officers shall you appoint at all your gates."[2] The discourse was based on the theme that emotions are the outcome of the intellect, the latter being their cause. The discourse elaborated on the passage,[3] "Fifty portals of understanding were created in the world." The fiftieth relates to Understanding proper; the other forty-nine correspond to the combinations of the emotion-attributes.[4] The commandment contained in the above quoted verse means, that in order that worship affect practice, every portal of emotion needs a 'judge' for its qualitative content, and an 'officer' for its quantitative content.

"My father was by then already writing glosses on his grandfather's [the Alter Rebbe's] discourses, besides interpretations for his own benefit based on *Midrash*, *Zohar*, and the

---

1. [The Torah is divided into portions read each Shabbat. Each week is therefore designated by the name of the parsha to be read the following Shabbat. *Shoftim* begins with Deut. 16:18. *Ki Tavo* begins with Deut. 26.]
2. Deut. 16:18.
3. *Rosh Hashana* 21b.
4. [Tr. Expl. Notes on *Emotion Powers*.]

writings of the Ari.[5] He was in doubt about some of the subjects in the discourse mentioned, and on Monday, 6 *Elul* 5564 (1804), was granted an audience to present his questions and have them clarified. The Alter Rebbe answered all his questions in order, and concluded by stating that each of the forty-nine portals has its own type of prayer. Prayer combines power with deed, as explained in a discourse of Rabbi DovBer, the Maggid of Mezritch, delivered on Shabbat Tavo 5528 (1768), beginning with the verse,[6] *V'shavta ad Havayeh Elokecha.*

"The Maggid explained, in that discourse, that the *avoda* of *teshuva* must attain a level at which *Havayeh*, transcendent Divinity beyond worlds, becomes *Elokecha—Elokim* being numerically equivalent to *hateva* [nature], and as we find,[7] *In the beginning* Elokim *created the heavens and the earth.* . . .

"All the disciples of the Maggid were profoundly stirred by the Maggid's words. The *tzadik* R. Meshulam Zusya of Anipoli asserted that he could not attain the lofty heights of such a *teshuva*; he would therefore break down *teshuva* into more

---

5. [Great sixteenth century Kabbalist.]
6. Deut. 30:2. ["You shall return to G-d you G-d." *V'shavta*, "you shall return," is an expression of *teshuva* ("return" or "repentance"), Two different names of G-d are used in the Hebrew verse: "you shall return to *Havayeh* (who is) *Elokecha*—your G-d." *Havayeh* is the Chasidic colloquialism used to indicate that the Name actually appearing in the Hebrew verse is the Tetragrammaton, the ineffable, unpronounced Name-of-Four-Letters.

"*Elokecha*" is a form of "*Elokim.*" *Havayeh* is indicative of G-d's transcendance; *Elokim*, of His immanence, descending, as it were, to create and vivify the world with His life-force. *Teshuva*, says the Maggid, must be to the point that the transcendent *Havayeh* becomes immanent and palpable.]
7. Gen. 1:1. [*Elokim* is associated with *creation*, as above.]

manageable components, for each letter of the word *teshuva* is the initial of a verse:

ת : *Tamim* – "Be sincere with the Eternal, your G-d."[8]
ש : *Shiviti* – "I have set G-d before me always."[9]
ו : *V'ahavta* – "Love your fellow as yourself."[10]
ב : *B'chol* – "In all your ways, know Him."[11]
ה : *Hatznei'a* – "Walk discreetly with your G-d."[12]

---

8. Deut. 18:13.
9. Psalms 16:8.
10. Lev. 19:18.
11. Proverbs 3:6.
12. Micah 6:8.

CHAPTER THIRTY

Five Methods in the *Avoda* of *Teshuva:* an explanation by Rabbi Shalom DovBer

"THE FIVE LETTERS of the word *teshuva*," concluded Rabbi Shmuel to Rabbi Shalom DovBer, "are five paths and methods in the *avoda* of *teshuva*, through which one arrives at actual repentance."

My father [Rabbi Shalom Dov-Ber] told me that the word *teshuva* is comprised of five letters, each signifying a path and a method in the *avoda* of *teshuva*, all to be realized, brought from potential to actual, through prayer.

He graciously elaborated on the five methods, of which I will discuss only the core briefly.

The first method of *avodat hateshuva:*
ת – *Tamim* . . . , "You shall be sincere with G-d." This represents the *avoda* of *teshuva* that comes through sincerity. Sincerity, or "wholeness," takes any number of forms and has many levels. In reference to *teshuva*, the highest form is wholeness of heart; as Torah says of Avraham,[1] "You found his heart faithful[2] before You,"—the wholeness of heart called earnestness.

---

1. Nehemiah 9:8.
2. [I.e. "whole."]

The second method of *avodat hateshuva*:

‫ש‬ – *Shiviti* . . . , "I have set G-d (*Havayeh*) before me always." *Havayeh* indicates the creation of the universe and creatures. Creation and the sustenance of it all is in a unique manner, *ex nihilo*.[3] This form of the *avoda* of *teshuva* results from one's constant awareness of the way in which the universe and all that is in it, is (constantly) brought into being.

The third method of *avodat hateshuva*:

‫ו‬ – *V'ahavta* . . . , "Love your neighbor as yourself." The Alter Rebbe taught that this love is a means to achieve "Love the Eternal, your G-d."[4] Our Sages declared,[5] "Whoever is pleasing to man is pleasing to G-d." This service of *teshuva* stems from goodness of heart.

The fourth method of *avodat hateshuva*:

‫ב‬ – *B'chol* . . . , "In all your ways, know Him." One who carefully observes all that happens to him and around him will see tangible evidence of G-d everywhere. Rabbi DovBer, the Mitteler Rebbe, pointed out the advantage, in this respect, of working folk over Torah students in that the former have more opportunity to witness the actual manifestations of G-d. This form of the service of *teshuva* comes from recognizing Divine Providence in the events of daily life.

---

3. [*Havayeh*, the Tetragrammaton, as is often mentioned in Chasidus, implies, etymologically, constancy of creation. "Who renews each day creation" (Prayer Book) indicates that the act of creation is continuous. See *Shaar Hayichud V'ha'emuna*, ch. 1. Hence, sustaining creation is no less a creative act than the original creation. "Unique" in the text emphasizes the infinite gap between created things and their Creator.]

4. Deut. 6:5.

5. *Avot* 3:10.

The fifth method of *avodat hateshuva*:

ה – *Hatznei'a* . . . , "Walk discreetly with your G-d." One must take care not to be conspicuous or ostentatious in the slightest. It is said, "Man should always be artful in piety."[6] This artfulness lies in the ability to conceal one's piety. We know that a number of the early Chasidim concealed their true selves, and when discovered were sincerely distressed. This is the *avoda* of *teshuva* that comes from *hatznei'a lechet*, being discreet.

In summation, the five methods of the *avoda* of *teshuva* comprise five avenues in Divine service. Each one of the five paths is a comprehensive avenue to be followed in all phases of man's service of G-d, not in repentance alone. Each one flows from the "well-spring flowing from the house of G-d"[7]— Chasidus. We can bring these paths from potentiality to actuality through the *avoda* of prayer, which is the foundation of effort and the pillar of deed. In this way, the Divine purpose of Creation, viz. "the Holy One, blessed be He, desired to have an abode in the lowest world" is fulfilled.

---

6. *Brachot* 17a.
7. Joel 4:18.

Book Three

On Learning Chasidus

TRANSLATOR'S FOREWORD
TO THE FIRST EDITION (1944)

THE ESSAY *ON Learning Chasidus* is another in a series of translations of Chabad literature. It is taken from *Kuntres Limud HaChasidus*, Kehot, Brooklyn, 1947. The series consists of profound expositions of some Chabad teachings, historical data, moral instruction, and personal experiences and memoirs of the authors.

On Learning Chasidus was written by the sixth Lubavitcher Rebbe, Rabbi Yosef Yitzchak Schneersohn. It discusses the urgency of studying this inner dimension (Chabad) of Torah, and demonstrates conclusively that with proper effort anyone can comprehend Chasidus. It may be regarded as a sequel to *On the Teachings of Chasidus*, an earlier essay of this series which addressed itself primarily to the basic character of Chasidus, and the place of worship in the total service of G-d. The reader is advised to examine that essay as an introduction to this work. He will probably discover that both require concentration and study, that mere perusal will not lead to understanding.

The footnotes were written by the Lubavitcher Rebbe, Rabbi Menachem M. Schneerson, excepting several short references and sources. Explanatory footnotes by the translator have been so marked.

"Translator's Explanatory Notes," reprinted from *On the Teachings of Chasidus*, have been appended to facilitate the study of these translations. It is suggested that the reader examine these Notes at the outset, and then refer to them as the necessity arises. The translator has also added a brief

Glossary of Hebrew terms, though the use of Hebrew has been kept to a minimum. The "Order of Succession," describing the leaders of Chasidus and Chabad in sequence, should allay confusion arising from names relating to different generations of Chabad leadership.

Zalman Posner
Nashville, Tennessee
Iyar, 5719 (May, 1959)

AUTHOR'S PROLOGUE

A CORRESPONDENT WROTE regarding a student who had reveiwed a Chasidic discourse mentioning the Rabbinical dictum,[1] "Israel arose in thought first." The reviewer had explained that the souls of Israel are considered pre-existent [i.e., *primary*] and cannot be described as *created*. The correspondent wonders whether the student understood the subject matter properly. Most probably, he thinks, the reviewer was mistaken since the term *pre-existent* should refer to none but G-d. Parenthetically, he also quotes *Tanya* [ch. 2] "[souls are] actually a part of G-d," maintaining that this is difficult to conceive. He concludes with the suggestion that perhaps it would be preferable not to discuss such abstract subjects at all, for they give ground to the allegation that Chasidim are irreverent. Besides, he remarks, mortals can never really understand these matters.

In summary, he feels that 1) the reviewer no doubt erred, since only G-d can be called *pre-existent*, 2) public discussion of such topics exposes Chasidim to criticisms of irreverence, and 3) mortals are incapable of clearly understanding such subjects.

---

1. *Bereishit Rabbah* 1:4. "Israel arose in thought [this is the text of numerous editions and mss.] . . . They said, 'The thought of Israel preceded all else.";
see *Likkutei Torah* on "*Shir HaShirim*," s.v. *Yonati*.

THE CORRESPONDENT'S ASSUMPTION that only G-d's existence can be termed primary, needs elucidation. Certainly, *pre-existence* properly refers only to G-d. All else is His production, either as emanations or as creatures.[1] This pertains, however, only to the more profound implications of the absolute adjective, *pre-existent*. In general usage though, the adjective may have varying applications, e.g., *Adam Kadmon*[2] [Primordial Man],[3] or the expressions *primary of all primaries*[4] and *primary thought.*[5]

Adjectives can be truly understood only in terms of their respective subjects. For example the adjective *echod* [one] is not constant in every context; it varies with its subject. "The L-rd is One,"[6] is hardly synonymous with "*one* day."[7] "One day" means *first* day, "one" being an enumeration, followed by "second day"; "one G-d" means *sole* G-d, the absolute One, or *yachid*.

Why then is He spoken of as One (*Echod*) rather than Sole (*Yachid*)? *Echod* indicates the unity and oneness of all beings in their source, the Almighty. This is indicated in the very letters

---

1. [See Explanatory Notes.]
2. *Tikkunei Zohar* beginning of ch. 70, and elsewhere.
3. [The Hebrew term *kadmon* is found in all the citations in this paragraph, including the one about Jewish souls. *Kadmon* has been translated as *pre-existent*, *primordial*, or *primary*, according to its context, since in every case it indicates precedence.]
4. Ibid.; *Eitz Chaim* I, a and b.
5. *Likkutei Torah. loc. cit.*; *Ateret Rosh*, "*Rosh Hashana*," ch. 5; *Imrei Bina*, "*Kriat Shema*," ch. 10; and elsewhere.
6. [Deut. 6:4.]
7. [Gen. 1:5.]

of the word *echod*: heaven and earth, which include all (spiritual and material) creation, are nullified before the Master of the Universe.[8]

Every adjective must similarly be examined for definition in accordance with its subject. *Primary* may thus refer to anything antecedent. If secondary subjects are in turn antecedent to tertiary subjects, the first may be called *primary of primaries* to indicate precedence to the next class, which is *primary* in terms of its successor, the third class.

---

8. [*Aleph* alludes to the Absolute One before Whom *chet* (material and spiritual worlds, from the lowliest to the loftiest) and *dalet* (the four corners of the mundane world) are as nothing.]

CHAPTER TWO

REGARDING THE FACULTIES of the soul, *primary of primaries* refers to the source of *will*, i.e. essence-will.[1] It precedes all powers, being the source of all, for "nothing stands in the way of will." Not only are emotion and intellect controlled by *will*, but even *delight* is affected by *will*, as is explained elsewhere at length, though it is inconclusive which is superior. (The maxim,[2] "There is none higher than delight," seems to conflict with "Nothing can obstruct will.")

In view of the above, we can understand why essence-will is called *primary of primaries*. For unlike an animal which stands on four feet, man's body is erect. The head is higher than the heart, and the heart and respiratory organs are higher than the digestive system. Man may be divided into three general categories: intellect, emotion and deed. Thought and speech are auxiliary powers, thought serving intellect, speech serving emotion.

The faculties and senses follow a pattern of sequence: emotion precedes speech, thought precedes emotion, and intellect precedes thought. Since each is antecedent to another, all are called *primary*. The beginning of the entire series is *will*, their antecedent and cause; consequently, it is called *primary of primaries*.

---

1. *Shaar HaYichud* [by the Mitteler Rebbe], ch. 16, *ff.*; *Ateret Rosh*, beginning; *Sefer HaMamaarim* 5701, s.v. *Tikku*; and elsewhere.
2. *Sefer Yetzira* 2:2 (according to many versions.)

We may now also understand the term *Adam Kadmon*, the first visage[3] emanating from G-d after the *condensation*. The words *Adam Kadmon* are used deliberately, each word contributing to the description: *Adam* (man) indicates order and system in composition, while *Kadmon* (primary) indicates that this level precedes all subsequent ones in the creative process as was explained above with regards to *will* preceding all else.

But all the foregoing refers to the definition of the adjective *primary* as related to creatures, i.e. in a figurative sense. True *primary existence* can refer only to G-d, the absolute Primary and Eternal. This is in accord with the saying, "Every primary is eternal, but not all eternals are primary."[4] Many beings, by decree of the Creator, may be eternal, though not a single one of them is primary. The term *primary* as used here refers to the absolute adjective, not to the variable meaning adjectives may assume. In its absolute sense, we learn from the citation, *primary* may be applied only to G-d.

All adjectives, then, possess both an essential or absolute meaning, and a figurative one. The essential meaning refers to G-d; its figurative meanings apply to creatures. Essential and figurative adjectives are found also in the sphere of intellect (wise, understanding, knowing), emotions (merciful, gracious, kindly, mighty, awesome), and similarly regarding adjectives describing unity, singularity and primacy: *one, sole,* and *primary*.

---

3. *Eitz Chaim* I, beginning.
4. *Yonat Elem*, Introduction; *Pelach HaRimon* 4:3.

CHAPTER THREE

THE REVIEWER OF the discourse mentioned above erred neither in comprehension nor in expression, his quotation being quite correct. The meaning of "Israel arose in thought" is that Jewish souls have pre-eminence over all creatures even in their manner of coming into being. All creatures, angels included, were created during the Six Days of Creation, their manner of creation was through Divine *speech*. "With ten expressions the world was created;"[1] "Birds that may fly"[2] refers to the angels.[3] Therefore the psalmist says, [4] "By the *word* of G-d the heavens were *made*", and[5] "Forever, O L-rd, Your *word* stands in the heavens,"[6] since Divine speech is equivalent to deed. "With the breath of His mouth all their hosts"[7] refers to celestial beings, all created through Divine speech.

But souls, though they too were called into being during the Six Days, were created in an entirely different manner. They were created by *thought*, and *thought* precedes *speech*. Thus souls derive from a higher state than *speech*, by which all other creatures were created. Hence, "Israel arose in thought." Among *sefirot*, *thought* is in the category of *wisdom*.[8] "Arose in thought" indicates *inner* (or higher) *wisdom*.

---

1. [*Avot* 5:1.]
2. [Gen. 1:20.]
3. Bereishit Rabbah 1:3.
4. [Psalms 33:6.]
5. [*Ibid.*, 119:89.]
6. Cf. Tanya, "Shaar HaYichud VehaEmunah."
7. [*Ibid.*, 33:6.]
8. Meorei Or 40:59; Likkutei HaShas, end of Brachot; see Likkutei Torah, loc. cit.

I will repeat a fundamental teaching of the Alter Rebbe, Rabbi Schneur Zalman, and his successors as it was expounded and frequently reiterated:

Maskil l'Eitan ha'Ezrachi (Psalms 89:1).[9]

Eitan is the essence of the soul as it cleaves to the Essence (of G-d), (*Eitan* is) a portion of G-d above. "The soul You have placed within me is *pure*; You *created* it; You *formed* it; You *breathed* it [into me].[10] The four [italicized] terms parallel the Four Worlds. The *Midrash*[11] enumerates five gradations of soul: *nefesh* (soul),[12] *ruach* (spirit), *neshama* (soul), *chaya* (living), and *yechida* (single).

The *Zohar*[13] reckons the first three and the fourth, *neshama l'neshama* (the soul of the soul), paralleling the four letters of *Havayah*. *Eitan* is the strength of the soul as manifested in the power of self-sacrifice. *Eitan* also means ancient,[14] not newly created . . . drawn from G-d's Essence. "The soul You have placed within me is pure" refers to the source of the soul as it is in the world of *Atzilut*. Emanation is a separation from the illumination of

---

9. Cf. *Likkutei Torah*, "*R'ei*"; *Mamaarim 5666*, s.v. "*Ve'Asita chag haShavuot*"; *Mamaarim 5688*, s.v. "*Amar Rebbi Yehoshua ben Levi...*"; and elsewhere.
10. Liturgy, Morning Blessings.
11. *Bereshit Rabbah* 14:9.
12. [The translations here are arbitrary, since English terminology cannot convey the fine differentiations between the gradations. At any rate the differences are unimportant for our purposes here.]
13. Vol. 1, p. 79b.
14. *Sotah* 46b.

the Infinite, the Emanator; it is not novel, but a revelation of the previously concealed.[15]

This is *maskil*, the source that creates and reveals the idea. *Maskil l'Eitan* (lit. "to *eitan*"), the revelation of *maskil* is only for *eitan*. And through the power of *maskil*, *eitan* arrives at *ha'ezrachi*,[16] the illumination of all powers and senses.

This lesson of the Alter Rebbe was repeated over the course of more than a century, through four generations of our Rebbes. Each of them in his day repeated the above with additional elucidation, elucidation that inspired all those souls living with the knowledge provided by the inner dimension of Torah.[17] How many thousands and tens of thousands of Chasidim—intellectuals, worshippers, and men of deeds[18]—found

---

15. Cf. *Mamaarim* 5666, s.v. "*Kedoshim*."
16. [*Ezrachi* means *illuminator*. For standard interpretation, cf. *Rashi* on Psalms 89:1, 88:1; Kings I, 5:11; Chronicles I, 2:6.]
17. [Further ch. 11; also, *On the Teachings of Chasidus*, ch. 1.]
18. [The study of Chasidus includes both intellectual aspects and applied ones. Frequently, the subject matter is profound and complex, a challenge to the finest mind. Utilizing the theoretics of Chasidus in inspired worship, developing and refining one's character, awakening love for G-d and reverence for Him, subordinating one's own will to the Higher Will and the needs of humanity—these are some directions that application of Chasidus may take.

By nature and endowment, some Chasidim are inclined to delving into the intricacies of Chasidic learning. They are known as *maskilim*, intellectuals. The forte of other Chasidim is the application of Chasidus, and they are known for their fervent and protracted worship. Generally, these *ovdim* (*oved*, singular) are more emotional and warmer than the *maskilim*.

The goal of Chasidus is not mere mental acquisition of its teachings, intellectual exercise *per se*. The individual must become improved by virtue of his scholarly attainments. "The true *oved* is a *maskil*; the true

inspiration in these holy words, and stimulation to serve G-d through study, service, and upright deeds with deep feeling and spirit.

Our Sages say,[19] "In the Hereafter there is neither food nor drink . . . but souls sit with their crowns on their heads and enjoy the splendor of the Divine Presence." Chasidus explains[20] that *splendor* refers to the radiance of the Torah and divine service engaged in by these souls in this life. Those holy souls of the Chasidim who during their lifetimes labored with body and soul in the study and application of Chasidus, now in the Higher World enjoy the light of their learning and prayer, rising continually in infinite elevations.

---

maskil is an *oved*," is an adage often repeated to emphasize the unity of learning and application.

Because of circumstances or limited capacities, some Chasidim were prevented from immersing themselves in the complexities of study, and devoting themselves to worship. Nevertheless, they fulfilled the practical demands of Torah and Chasidus in sincere piety, earnest prayer, refinement in their relations with others, and meticulous and warmhearted observance of a Jew's obligations, according to their abilities. They are known as "men of deeds."]

19. *Brachot* 17a. The text there reads, "The *righteous* sit . . . ."
20. *Tanya*, ch. 39; *Likkutei Torah*, s.v. "*V'shavta*," 2.

CHAPTER FOUR

THE TWO OBJECTIONS of the correspondent (on the grounds of irreverence and the incapacity of mortals to clearly understand these subjects) are not limited to the subject "Israel arose in thought" alone. They are as relevant to most of the subject matter of Chasidus. These claims are similar to the anti-Chasidic arguments proposed by the moderate *mitnagdim* of earlier generations.

The opponents of the ideology and practices of Chasidus were of two types. The first group bitterly opposed the movement and was unreasonably suspicious of Chasidim. A second more patient group was cognizant of the principles of intellectual fairness. The acts of the first group need no elaboration here. For the second group, however, the above-mentioned objections and other similar allegations formed the basis of their antipathy to Chasidus.

During the first period of the birth and expansion of Chabad Chasidus, i.e., during the lifetime of the Alter Rebbe, the second group was quiescent, while the first active and vociferous. After the victories of 1798 and 1801,[1] the first group was discredited and the second began to take form. During the next ten years (until 1812) they carried on disputes and debates with the Chasidim.

Undeniably, in a number of instances they weakened the study of Chasidus, particularly among the common householder

---

1. For details on the first arrest, see *Yud Tes Kislev*, Brooklyn, 1941. On the second arrest, see further.

who was mainly occupied with personal affairs and who had precious little time to apportion between Talmud or the like and Chasidus. In most Chasidic strongholds the *mitnagdim* exploited epistles[2] of the Alter Rebbe himself ("To begin with blessing," and "Ten who study Torah") and other citations that stress the importance of Talmud study. They pointed out that the Rebbe too holds that the study of Talmud and *halacha* must be rigorously observed before anything else.

During these crucial years many students of the Alter Rebbe's *chedarim*[3] travelled extensively throughout the land; local and regional committees were formed to carefully observe developments. The *mitnagdim*, in turn, sent secret emissaries into the Chasidic camp. It was secret, internal warfare, neither group eager for publicity. Then, (in the summer of 1812) the Franco-Russian War erupted throwing the world into turmoil. The Rebbe fled from his home in Liadi, and more than a year elapsed before his son and successor, Rabbi DovBer, the Mitteler Rebbe, settled in Lubavitch.

---

2. [*Tanya, Iggeret HaKodesh*, Epistles 1, and 23.]
3. His students were divided into three groups called *chedarim*, seminars. See *On the Teachings of Chassidus*, page 78.

CHAPTER FIVE

WITH THE END of the war, the *mitnagdim* renewed their activities, dispatching men to influence the Chasidim not to form bonds with the Mitteler Rebbe as his Chasidim. Though their efforts were soon obviously unsuccessful, they still entertained hopes. Even with the Mitteler Rebbe in Lubavitch, they felt that they could devise some stratagem against him, knowing him to be self-effacing and placatory.

This second generation of Chabad leadership began in the midst of post-war chaos. The provinces of White Russia and Lithuania were greatly affected by the Mitteler Rebbe's presence among them in Lubavitch. It was widely known that the Alter Rebbe had been active in the recent struggle, and that as a result, the government and nobility were sympathetic toward the Chasidim.

Most important for the morale of the Chasidim, upon assuming formal leadership of the Chasidim in 1814, the Mitteler Rebbe issued unequivocal orders that the Chasidim of White Russia build their own synagogues. Under no condition were they to enter the synagogues of *mitnagdim*. Violators would be punished with expulsion from the Chasidic fraternity. In this way the influence of *mitnagdim* would be minimized.

On occasion, he instructed Chasidim residing in towns without a quorum of Chasidim, to pray in solitude and to listen to the Torah reading[1] from outside the synagogue. I well

---

1. [The Torah is read on Shabbat morning and afternoon, and Monday and Thursday mornings, when a quorum of ten men are present for prayer.]

remember a Chasid from Vitebsk who had lived in Lida at that time. For the five years he lived in Lida, he never prayed in a synagogue except for the two months a year that he spent in Lubavitch.[2] The Mitteler Rebbe ordered all Chasidim to refrain from any sort of discussion with mitnagdim; the younger Chasidim received stern warnings to this effect. These drastic measures isolated the opposing camps sharply and completely. The moderate mitnagdim were now almost convinced that their ambitions of discouraging the study of Chasidus were doomed.

One glimmer of hope remained. The mitnagdim hoped to develop a schism among the Chasidim through the disciples of the Alter Rebbe, Rabbi Aaron Strasheler and Rabbi Shmuel Freidesh.[3] But even this desperate attempt was promptly counteracted.

As soon as the Mitteler Rebbe settled in Lubavitch, he assembled hundreds of gifted young scholars where they devoted themselves diligently to studying Chasidus and reviewing his regular Shabbat mamaarim. A rule was instituted that forbade any young man from remaining in Lubavitch for more than two, or in special cases three, months. En route home, each young man was required to spend a day or two in every town he passed, reviewing in each place the discourses he had learned in Lubavitch. The Chasidim of every city, town and village in White Russia agreed to supply all wayfarers to and from Lubavitch with food and lodgings.

---

2. [After the death of the Alter Rebbe in 1812, the Mitteler Rebbe, his son and successor, setttled in Lubavitch, which remained the seat of Chabad for 102 years. It is customary that Chasidim visit the Rebbe for varying lengths of time, especially at holiday seasons.]

3. They led an abortive movement to draw Chasidim away from the Mitteler Rebbe. See Beit Rebbe, ch. 26.

These measures effectively united the Chasidim and contributed to the extended influence of Chasidus.

CHAPTER SIX

AFTER THE ALTER Rebbe returned from his second arrest in S. Petersburg (1801) and settled in Liadi, he instituted a new system of expounding Chasidus. Previous discourses were generally succinct, and the *bi'urim*, or "elucidations," were also of extreme brevity. Now he began delivering lengthy discourses with interpretations and super-interpretations. Frequently he delivered the same discourse with three or four "interpretations," each uniquely profound in content.

This release of 1801 had even more far-reaching beneficial effects for Chasidus than did the release of 1798. Though only the first arrest involved prison, still the charges were more serious the second time. The charges in 1798 were leveled primarily against the Rebbe personally—his alleged ambitions of becoming a monarch over the Land of Israel, recruiting followers and raising funds toward this goal, plotting revolution, and so forth. In contrast, the charges in 1801 were aimed primarily against Chasidic ideology.

In 1798 the Alter Rebbe allowed only intercessors and their aides to come to S. Petersburg. In 1801, however, he permitted all his Chasidim to visit him, and from many communities, delegations came to inquire about the Rebbe's welfare. Three weeks before his release from Taini Soviet[1] in 1801 the Chasidim learned that they had won a decisive victory and that the Rebbe's release was imminent. Only due to the formality of royal authorization and consent of the Senate was there a delay.

---

1. [Lit. "secret council"; the prison where the Alter Rebbe was held.]

In contrast to the imprisonment in the Petropavli[2] fortress in 1798, the confinement in Taini Soviet was comfortable. Taini Soviet was more commodious than an ordinary prison, and much more pleasant than the Petropavli fortress. Since the Rebbe was recognized by the officials as an unusual personality, he was treated with utmost respect. He was permitted to have any books he desired, and to make his own arrangements for food.

One day the commandant of the prison told him that the verdict was favorable to Chasidus; the Rebbe himself was also exonerated and would be permitted to continue teaching Chasidus without interference by the Government. Until the Czar and the Senate would officially approve the verdict however, he would have to remain in Taini Soviet. Since he was legally free, guards would no longer be posted and visitors would have unimpeded access to him. An apartment with four spacious rooms was assigned for his use in the outer court, pending the clearance of his papers and his return home.

Immediately, the Rebbe moved to his new quarters, and within a few hours the Chasidim learned of the developments. Messengers were sent to Liozna, the Rebbe's home, and to all Chasidic communities. One of the rooms was designated a synagogue, a Torah scroll was brought, and services were conducted regularly. Until his final release, the Rebbe lived just as in Liozna.

A great many wondrous stories have been recounted about that last period in Taini Soviet, but this is not the place for them, except to note that the Rebbe's joy was unbounded.

---

2. [The Peter & Paul fortress, in S. Petersburg.]

accommodate 300 people, and he addressed his Chasidim. The Chasidim were surprised and amazed by this new practice. Some of them had known the Rebbe for twenty-five years and had never known him to designate a daily period to spend with Chasidim. Besides, the content of his talks, and the stories he told, were extraordinary.

The Rebbe's demeanor those days spent in the apartment at Taini Soviet, his narratives and talks, were permeated with unequaled happiness. His sheer joy could not be understood; it could only be felt. Some things cannot be grasped by the frigid mind; they can be perceived only by one with feeling, by a refined, warm heart. The Rebbe, the *"Tzemach Tzedek,"* Rabbi Menachem Mendel, in discussing this period with his son Rabbi Shmuel, said that the Rebbe's conduct was like that of the *Baal Toke'ah*[3] after sounding the *shofar* on Rosh Hashana. According to Kabbalah, the *Baal Toke'ah* is to return to his seat facing the congregation, each looking at the other. This mutual look of affection, symbolic of love and unity, counteracts any opposition to the Divine mercies elicited by the *shofar* blowing.[4]

"While in Taini Soviet," the *"Tzemach Tzedek"* told his son, Rabbi Shmuel, "my grandfather was the intercessor for Divine mercies for Chasidim and Chasidus. He alone was aware of the grave danger hovering over the teachings of the Baal Shem Tov and Chabad Chasidus. I remember well the two occasions when my grandfather was taken to S. Petersburg. The first time he

---

3. [The one who blows the *shofar*.]

4. [The *shofar* arouses and expresses the Jewish people's contrition, the repentance that elicits Divine mercies. In the heavenly court, where men's fate is decided, the pleas for mercy are countered by insistence on severity in judgment.]

was transported in a black coach used for criminals, and escorted by armed guards. The second time two commissioned officers came with their aides and notified the Rebbe that they desired to speak with him. If he had no time that day, they said, they would come tomorrow.

"Before the appointment, the Rebbe sent Reb Chaim Zalman, a leading citizen of Liozna who spoke Russian fluently, to accompany the officers to the meeting place. After spending some three hours with the Rebbe, the officers departed. The following week, the Alter Rebbe traveled to S. Petersburg as he had assured the officers he would.

"More than once the Rebbe told me of the peril to Chasidus: 'The first arrest was directed against me personally. But I had no fears, since in over thirty years of work I had succeeded in training a number of students with an extensive knowledge of Chasidus. Even though my son, your father-in-law [Rabbi DovBer], was still quite young, I was confident that my disciples would assist him. On the other hand, the second accusation was directed mainly against Chasidus. Though the teaching of Chasidus was not prohibited all during the proceedings, and though my son, your father-in-law, was already a most capable leader and Chasidic educator, still I was deeply concerned, because the opposition was so powerful.'

"The trial's conclusion and the exoneration of Chasidus explains the great joy the Alter Rebbe enjoyed, as Chasidim visited him in Taini Soviet as they had done in Liozna."

Rabbi Shmuel once remarked to his son, Rabbi Shalom DovBer, that he read a transcript of the narratives and discourses delivered in Taini Soviet. Unfortunately, these notes were all consumed in the fire of 1856 in Lubavitch, but he repeated much of the material to Rabbi Shalom DovBer.

When the approved papers arrived, the Alter Rebbe was informed that he could leave Taini Soviet. For about three months, however, he was to remain in S. Petersburg. This last stipulation dismayed the Rebbe. He knew that there was a proposal before the authorities that he be required to establish permanent residence in the capital. He was actually to be given a measure of assistance by the Treasury to carry on his work publicly and freely, yet he was to remain in S. Petersburg.

From the time that the Rebbe had been confined to his own quarters in Taini Soviet many Chasidim came to S. Petersburg. When he left the prison-apartment for his own dwelling rented in town, hundreds of Chasidim accompanied his coach. The procession created quite an impression in the city.

Prince Lubomirski, a high official and confidant of the Czar, was in S. Petersburg at the time. He happened to be sitting on a balcony when the Rebbe's coach, followed by an ever-increasing crowd, passed. The Prince noticed the Rebbe's holy face and was very intrigued. In his official capacity he was acquainted with the accusations and the case, but he had taken only a cursory interest in the matter. Now that he witnessed the honor accorded the Chasidic leader, he wanted to meet him personally. A few days later he sent word to the Rebbe requesting an audience. The Rebbe set a time for the appointment.

Among the Chasidim then in the city were many lessees of Lubomirski's estate in Mogilev. One was Avraham Kruler, a personal and respected friend of the Prince. Avrohom visited the Prince and described the Rebbe's eminence to him, explaining the reverence with which scores of thousands of Chasidim regarded the Alter Rebbe. He mentioned that the Chasidim were troubled, since the Rebbe's residence in S. Petersburg would preclude their frequent visits to him as had been their custom when he was in Liozna. He told the Prince incidentally, that the Rebbe's choice of residence would bring economic benefits to the chosen community. In addition to the honor accruing to the lord of the city where the Rebbe would reside, the townspeople would benefit financially and would be able to pay higher taxes with greater ease. Avrohom flattered the Prince and declared that if the Prince so desired, the Prince could, no doubt, influence the Crown to permit the Rebbe to live in one of the Prince's own cities.

Later, when Lubomirski visited the Rebbe, Lubomirski told the Rebbe that if he would consent to live in Dubrovna or Liadi, two of Lubomirski's estates, permission to leave S. Petersburg permanently would be forthcoming. The Alter Rebbe agreed and chose Liadi. Lubomirski ordered the manager of his estates in Liadi to construct homes for the Rebbe and his family. All new settlers were to be given building materials for homes and stables, free of charge. The count further asked Avrohom Kruler that he supervise the construction of the homes for the Rebbe and his household.

While still in S. Petersburg, the Rebbe sent emissaries to all the Chasidic communities. These men were to bolster the study and practices of Chasidus, and they discharged their assignments competently. When the Rebbe left the capital for Liadi, a journey that lasted two weeks, he was accompanied by thousands. It is said that five thousand people entered Liadi with him.

The *"Tzemach Tzedek"* described the years the Alter Rebbe spent in Liadi as an unbroken chain of gratification. Most of his pupils covered the country in a campaign to disseminate Chasidus and promote Chasidic practice. (Often, they were opposed by representatives of the *mitnagdim* who endeavored strenuously to weaken the influence of the Rebbe's men.) In Liadi, the Rebbe permitted selected pupils to expound upon various teachings of Chasidus. This innovation gave further impetus and encouragement to the Chasidim.

The Alter Rebbe instructed his son, Rabbi DovBer, to transcribe the weekly Shabbat exposition. A remarkably swift scribe, the Mitteler Rebbe usually had his copy completed by Sunday evening, and then scores of copies were made and sent to all Chasidic communities. All these developments considerably buoyed the spirit of Chasidim.

CHAPTER SEVEN

INEVITABLY, THE NAPOLEONIC War disrupted the studies disastrously and gave many reason for worry. With the arrival of the Mitteler Rebbe, however, his settling in Lubavitch and the issuance of his instructions described above (ch. 5), *Anash* was again aroused, and the glory of Chasidus and Chasidim uplifted.

Under the leadership of the Mitteler Rebbe the number of Chasidim doubled and tripled. His young disciples possessed scholarly qualities—many were also proficient orators—and the Rebbe's discourses themselves contained broad explanations to facilitate understanding by the average layman. Elder Chasidim related, that during his first year of leadership, an additional fifteen thousand Jews became Chasidim in White Russia alone, and during his second year (1815) all of Chernigev province embraced Chabad.

Throughout his leadership, Rabbi DovBer strove to avoid encounters between Chasidim and *mitnagdim*. He cautioned his disciples to maintain peace. If ever a conflict did erupt, he censured the Chasidim and punished them by forbidding visits to Lubavitch for appropriate periods of time. As a result, debates rarely occurred. The *mitnagdim* persisted in denouncing Chasidim, but they were ignored, since the Chasidim were forbidden to resort to counter-arguments and justification.

In all of his communal activities, governmental or general, the Mitteler Rebbe did have contact with the *mitnagdim*, but only on communal matters relating to the improvement of the material welfare of the Jewish people. No word was ever uttered concerning Torah or Chasidus.

CHAPTER EIGHT

DURING THE THIRD generation of Chabad leaders, namely under the leadership of the *"Tzemach Tzedek,"* Rabbi Menachem Mendel, the first fifteen years (1828-1843) offered no opportunity for conflict between Chasidim and *misnagdim.* The *"Tzemach Tzedek"* devoted himself during this period to teaching his disciples, and did not engage in any public activities. In 1842, when he was appointed to the Rabbinical Commission in S. Petersburg,[1] he met for the first time with *mitnagdim* to plan together for the impending Commission.

He had made frequent visits (1832-3, 1836-41) to Chasidic communities in White Russia, visiting Minsk and Vilna. Wherever he came, *mitnagdim* joined in according him great honor and attended his Chasidic lectures. He granted them audiences to discuss Torah law as they requested. Nonetheless, there was no affinity. Any exchange of views was fleeting and incidental to the Torah discussions. Not until the meetings for the Commission did they unite to work in common cause for the general welfare.

This new-found accord and cooperation between the respective leaders of the Chasidic and *mitnagdic* factions delighted both camps equally, since the reputation of the *"Tzemach Tzedek"* had long since (from about 1829) penetrated and grown among the *mitnagdim.* To arrange the logistics of the Commission, a special committee was formed in Vitebsk, composed of philanthropists from both groups. The first

---

1. Cf. *Admur HaTzemach Tzedek Utnuat HaHaskala*, Brooklyn, 1944. [English rendition, Kehot, Brooklyn.]

meeting of the *"Tzemach Tzedek"* and Rabbi Yitzchak of Volozhin, the leader of the *mitnagdim*, left a strong impression on Rabbi Yitzchak, and a favorable impression on the *"Tzemach Tzedek."* The venerable Yitzchak Rubashov, who was then in S. Petersburg and had attended the *"Tzemach Tzedek,"* told me that observers remarked that the meeting proved to the *mitnagdim* that Chasidim were scholars, and convinced the Chasidim that *mitnagdim* were pious.

This rapprochement and communal cooperation had salutary effects on the general relationships between the Chasidim and *mitnagdim*. In some places the union became personal and families joined in marriage—the antagonists were reunited.

CHAPTER NINE

BY THIS TIME the quarrelsome *mitnagdim* were all but repudiated; at any rate the animosity was limited to the hard-core of bitter foes. The second group (see above ch. 4)—those who dispassionately questioned the principles of Chasidus, believing that they were doing so sincerely, not maliciously—became active. Nonetheless, though presented calmly and rationally, their questions were still deprecatory of Chasidus. All their questions and observations revolved on two points: 1) the objection to engaging in "esoterics," and 2) the incapacity of the human mind to understand such subjects clearly, leading to the possibility of misconception and consequent calamitous results.

Thank G-d, none of these objections made any impression, for there were always Chasidim of stature who completely dispelled every doubt and objection.

But all these debates took place more than fifty years ago. Then questions were posed[1] regarding the need for Chasidus and the benefits of the Chasidic lifestyle. The past fifty years

---

1. Cf. *On the Teachings of Chasidus*; Introduction to *Kuntres Etz HaChayim*, Brooklyn, 1946. [In reply to a letter about the necessity for Chasidus (for is not *Musar* study sufficient for piety, and besides, the study of Talmud and related works should be the student's sole interest), Rabbi Yosef Yitzchak Schneersohn writes: "Whoever studies Torah without love and fear (of G-d) cannot arrive at the true intent of the Giver of the Torah. . . . (After studying Chasidus according to the suggested program) you will be convinced that the Inner Torah alone can make an elixir of life of the revealed Torah, and that the study of Chasidus leads to fulfillment of the positive commandment of the Unity of the Creator, to love and revere. . . ." (p.13).]

have proven conclusively that Chasidus is indispensable in Jewish life.

Analogously, the study of *Musar* in *yeshivot* had been strenuously opposed by contemporary *gaonim*. Late in 1895, I was present at a meeting of the leading scholars of the day, including most of the Lithuanian *yeshiva* deans. The question of formal *Musar* study arose. Out of respect, I will refrain from mentioning the names of the opponents to this program and their outspoken opposition. Experience has vindicated *Musar* study. It is a verifiable fact that every *yeshiva* with a program of *Musar* study, especially those headed by a *menahel ruchni* (spiritual mentor), produced more righteous and G-d-fearing pupils than those *yeshivot* without such *Musar* sessions.

The proof is evident and alive. A generation ago the necessity for the study and practice of *Musar* principles was recognized and so, with G-d's help, they succeeded in training pious students. In our own day we see that the study of Chasidus is critically necessary for most *yeshiva* students. With His help we shall soon see the bright day when all truly upright *yeshivot* will institute the study and practice of Chasidus.

CHAPTER TEN

IN REGARD TO the two questions posed at the beginning of this letter: I am most reluctant to discuss at length what has already been often repeated in authentic narratives and published debates. One should denounce, in no uncertain terms, those who persist in this policy of casting doubts and instilling fears. Did I not know the questioner's sincerity and piety I would employ a tone of admonition; I would censure him for advocating the fallacious contention that has historically been detrimental to the service of G-d, and is so regretted in the True World now by erstwhile proponents of that policy. But I am aware of the questioner's earnestness and cognizant of the effects of his environment. His views have their source among the second group of *mitnagdim*, and are shared erroneously by truly religious and learned *mitnagdim* until this day, so I feel obligated to reply, if briefly.

The first objection, that public discussion of the subtle topics of Chasidus may lead to the accusation that we are, G-d forbid, irreverent of His honor, can be divided under four headings:

1) not to engage in the "esoteric," 2) concern for public opinion, 3) fear of stimulating accusations, and 4) public discussion.

The proper procedure for mastering any intellectual subject is preparatory presentation of its general principles, and then, orderly exposition of their details.

The first commandment[1] given at Sinai was *Anochi*, "I am. . . ."
(Exodus 20:2), the commandment of *emunah*. Maimonides
writes, יסוד היסודות ועמוד החכמות "The foundation of foundations
and the pillar of wisdoms (note: the acronym in these words, he
hints at the Tetragrammaton. Faith must be in Him Who
transcends nature, for His relationship with His people is super-
natural.)[2] is to know that there is a First Existence, the Cause of
every existence. All existing in heaven and earth and between
them, do not exist but for His true existence."[3]

I have elsewhere[4] written that one must apply reason and
understanding to this faith; Maimonides says *to know* rather

---

1. Cf. Derech Mitzvotecha, "Ha'amonat Elokut," 1 and 2.
2. Op. cit. "Achdut Hashem."
3. Mishne Torah, Yesodai HaTorah, 1:1.
4. *HaTamim* I, p. 25: [After a lengthy definition of the requirements of
   the obligation "to know", the Rebbe continues: This then is the duty
   of "You shall know" (Deut. 4:39)—to labor with the mind to
   understand G-dliness to the best of one's abilities. One must
   understand so well that it (the knowledge that G-d is G-d in the
   heavens above and the earth below, there is nothing else) becomes
   "close to his heart" (ibid.), that his heart is aroused with Love and
   Fear of G-d expressed in fulfillment of practical duties and study of
   Torah. This duty, knowledge of Torah and G-dliness through the
   interpretations of Chasidus, is so vital because it endows religious
   living with inner spirit.
   All the preceding (reference is to the text, here untranslated) is in
   refutation of the two arguments that 1) mortals have no dealings with
   esoteric lore, and 2) not every mind can grasp these studies. Both
   arguments are intellectually frivolous; it is humiliating for a thinking
   person even to utter them. Any idea in any field is "esoteric" and
   "hidden" until one studies it, and without preparation the mind
   cannot entertain any idea.
   Many non-students of Torah excuse themselves with the complaint that
   "their minds cannot assimilate Torah." In their worldly affairs their minds
   are ingenious and creative, but the attraction of the worldly life is so

than *to believe*. This expression thus indicates that comprehension of this subject is in fact possible, and that whoever understands as much as he can will have a strengthened faith in what is beyond his grasp. This is the true meaning of faith.

The commandment *Anochi* was given to all Israel equally. Every Jew is obligated to perform this positive commandment, each according to his intellectual abilities. It follows that one who can fulfill this duty but fails to do so, violates a positive commandment. One whose mind is incapable of understanding may perform the duty of believing through accepting tradition. But one with a strong and healthy intellect cannot discharge his obligation through passively accepting traditional belief; as a personal obligation, it (the knowledge Maimonides demands) cannot be delegated to another. Whoever neglects this duty comes within the meaning of the passage,[5] "The commandments of the L-rd he denied."

Those who rationalize and claim that we have no business with the "esoteric," lean on a broken rod. Besides the intrinsic error of their contention (Why indeed have they no business

---

enticing that they are not ashamed to deprecate themselves where Torah is concerned. Were a merchant to be told by his fellow that he is inept and lacking in business acumen, he would be insulted and furious at the other's audacity. But when one remarks at his ignorance of Torah, instead of the fool being insulted he actually uses his ignorance as an excuse for not studying!

All this is equally true of the study of Chasidus. Certainly! Before one studies Chasidus it is mysterious, and without the preparatory work Chasidus demands, the mind cannot understand. . . .]

Cf. *"Haamonat Elokut,"* where Maimonides includes this in the commandment *Anochi*.

5. Num. 15:31.

with the "esoteric"? Who absolved them?),[6] Chasidus is not "hidden" or supra-intellectual. Chasidus is a coherent systematized study, patterned on the process of developed ideas that, in reality, clarifies many of the "hidden" subjects of Kabbalah.

It has been explained at length that Chasidus does more than enlighten one in the knowledge of the Written and Oral Law.[7] It does more than imbue one with enthusiasm in the performance of the *duties of the heart* which are as delineated in their own terms as are the practical precepts.[8] In addition, Chasidus demonstrates a manner of conduct and social intercourse according to criteria of perfection inconceivable without its guidance and teachings.

A cursory familiarity with Chasidus is sufficient to know that many of its subjects are both comprehensible intellectually and efficacious in improving moral attributes. Individuals incapable of grasping the intellectual aspects of Chasidus can perceive the admonitions and moral instruction of the study. Chasidus has a profound influence on their religious and personal conduct. Scores of thousands of devout people in every generation are the produce of Chasidus, which animated their souls and those of their families.

The accomplishments of Chasidus are common knowledge. It has had great effect on scholars, broadening their native abilities and expanding the scope of their learning. Those of

---

6. Introduction by Rabbi Chaim Vital to *Shaar HaHakdamot* (reprinted in Supplements to *Kuntres Etz HaChayim*), ruling noted at the beginning of Zohar; *Shomer Emunim*, Debates 1, 29, ff.
7. ["Written Law" refers to the Pentateuch and "Oral Law" describes the later works that were originally transmitted orally.]
8. *HaTamim*, loc. cit.

lesser talents have felt its effectiveness in improved understanding of Torah and inspiration to finer fulfillment of religious teachings. Even those simple folk unable to appreciate Torah wisdom were left with an indelible imprint in their love for Torah and Torah living, love of fellow Jews, and a deep-rooted strengthened faith.

Now then, one cannot be absolved even from the study of Kabbalah by pleading that "we have no business with the hidden," for how can one argue against studying any aspect of Torah? Regarding Chasidus, this argument is especially irrelevant and specious. To its students, Chasidus reveals itself as an orderly definitive discipline bringing essential benefits in fulfillment of both practical and "heart" duties, enlightening its students with a comprehension of G-d's Unity. Chasidus gives its students a firm footing in ordering all their affairs. The four divisions of the first observation may be considered refuted.

CHAPTER ELEVEN

NOW FOR THE second objection, viz., that mortals can never clearly grasp these concepts. In general, the argument "impossible" is feeble. No one dealing with ideas may say "impossible" at the outset; he would never attempt to learn. It is patently impossible for anyone with mediocre intellectual gifts to comprehend Talmud as did Rashi, the Tosafists, Maimonides, and Rosh.[1] Is that a reason for not even attempting to study and understand as much as possible? It is unnecessary to elaborate so obvious a point. This irresponsible objection to Chasidus is trivial compared to the havoc wreaked on the superficial student subscribing to that policy. One could as logically declare, "I cannot be a Solomon, so why bother studying at all?"

Granted, Chasidus is a particularly profound study, concerned with intangible, delicate concepts. The subjects of Chasidus are of a spiritual, abstract nature, and even the illustrations and explanations are removed from the realm of tangible, sensory perception. Some are impossible of perception as the term is used in human understanding.

In Chasidus, as in the Revealed Torah,[2] there are gradations. In addition, Chasidus has its own *PaRDeS*: understanding through literal meaning, indication, homily, and esoteric meaning.[3]

---

1. Commentators and codifiers of the Talmud.
2. Cf. On the Teachings of Chasidus, ch. 1.
3. [Four planes of understanding. *PaRDeS* is an acrostic for פשט רמז דרוש סוד
   pshat, remez, drush and *sod*.]

Revealed Torah in general has two characteristics: 1) it is the exposition of individual precepts in all their particular ramifications, 2) in those portions that have no relevance to practical law, it possesses the distinctive quality of being G-d's Torah. Chasidus, the "Inner Torah," also has two general characteristics:

1) Chasidus interprets the laws expounded in Revealed Torah according to their "inner" meaning, each topic and law as it is in essence. Hence Chasidus is called "Inner Torah," the inner dimension of the Revealed Torah.

2) Chasidus has its own particular field of study, the systematic elucidation of such subjects as the purpose of the soul's descent into the body, service of G-d, etc.

In Talmud study, we find greater ease in mastering a complex and difficult practical law than a less involved theoretical discussion. Comprehension comes through tangible association; a law, though involved with the most complex reasoning, has tangible associations to seize upon. Theory, though perhaps in itself less complex, lacks tangible associations, and is therefore less accessible.

The most abstruse talmudic theory, be it concerned with purity or sacrificial practice or civil or festival law, has in its very subject (impurities, offerings, demands and counter-arguments, Shabbat property definitions) tangible associations. We are familiar with the physical existence of the subject. When Chasidus treats those subjects in its terms, then the very existence of the subject is not readily conceived. In Revealed Law, since the subject is palpable, we can grasp the detailed complicated law; in Chasidus, since the subjects are of an abstract nature lacking tangible associations, comprehension is more difficult.

CHAPTER TWELVE

LET US EXAMINE a Talmudic law in the light of Chasidus—
the law of the נגע nega, the "affliction" that is suspected leprosy.[1]

The moral attributes or emotions (kindness,[2] severity, etc.)
are lower than, and caused by, the intellect, a composite in turn
of *concept* and *comprehension*—concept being antecedent to,
and higher than, *comprehension*. When *comprehension* exceeds
or overshadows the *concept*, the effect on the attributes, their
derivative, is (נגע) *nega*, the opposite of (ענג) *oneg*,[3] "delight."

When the attributes are under the influence of the superior,
concept, then the attributes coalesce; they act in cooperation, so
to speak. They become modified, rather than operating without
counter-balance. Severity is tempered with kindness, forming
kindness-in-severity, and vice-versa.

When this superior light is absent, then each attribute
possesses its particular character without modification and acts
independently, without incorporating aspects from the other
attributes. Not only do they not fortify one another, but they
are exclusive and divided. The results are inevitably
undesirable—*nega*, affliction, the antithesis of *oneg*, delight.

---

1. *Zohar* III, 49b; *Etz Chaim*, "Leah V'Rachel," 7; *Likutei Torah*, "Tazria"
   and "Metzora"; *Derech Mitzvotecha*. "*Tumat Hametzora*"; *Kuntres*
   18 Elul 5703, p.15.
2. [All terms used in these two paragraphs are discussed in the
   Translator's Explanatory Notes.]
3. [The different combinations of the same letters, allude to their
   antithetical nature.]

Only through the influence of *concept* (*chochma*) can there be *oneg*. The Talmud[4] describes the countenance of R. Abahu as shining (with delight) when he discovered a new teaching. "The wisdom of man illumines his visage"[5] with the discovery of a new thought. The absence of *chochma* is followed by *nega*.

The prescribed Torah procedure in the event of a *nega* is, "He shall be brought before the priest,"[6] effort, strenuous effort, must be exerted to receive the enlightenment of *concept*, the higher influence.

An example from the laws of sacrifices:[7] אדם מכם כי יקריב קרבן להי "When a man will bring of you an offering to G-d..."[8] The text should preferably have read, "When a man of you will bring." The interpretation is, "When a man will bring" (note: the Hebrew יקריב *yakriv* also implies "approach")—i.e., when one desires to approach the service of G-d, "of you an offering to G-d"—the initial step must be "of you," of yourselves, the idea of approach and sacrifice being the offering of one's abilities and faculties to Him.

Parenthetically, Reb Alter Yechiel, a Liozna teacher, once told my great-uncle Rabbi Boruch Shalom[9] that he had taught Talmud to the Mitteler Rebbe on a profound level when his pupil was a lad of ten. Reb Alter Yechiel once asked him the meaning of the quoted verse with the observation noted. the

---

4. *Yerushalmi*, Shabbat 8: 1.
5. Eccl. 8:1.
6. Lev. 13:2.
7. Cf. Kuntres 43, "Ushavtem," Succot 5701.
8. Lev. 1:2.
9. Son of Rabbi Menachem Mendel, the *Tzemach Tzedek*; cf. *Sicha, Pesach* 5703, sec. 63.

Mitteler Rebbe replied, "*When a man brings of you*—when one offers to G-d all he has, then he is *an offering to G-d* (*Havayeh*)—higher than the nature He has endowed in time and space. This person is not merely an offering to *Elokim*, symbolic of Nature."[10]

In civil law we find, "Two grasping a *talit*," a garment,[11] [each one claims, "I found it," each one claims, "It is all mine"]. *Talit* refers to encompassing light, the spark of good implanted within material objects. When two grasp a *talit*, i.e. both perform a *mitzvah* with a physical object, they release and clarify the spark of good imprisoned within that object. They redeem the spark from "exile" in matter, and elevate the matter itself from its intrinsic crassness, since the material object was an instrument for fulfilling the Divine plan of creation.

Now, the souls of the two who performed the *mitzvah*, upon their ascent to the True World, seize the *talit*, the spark that had been in the physical object, the material having already been purified and the spark elevated through the performance of the *mitzvah*. "One says, *I found it*"; he insists that *his* efforts redeemed the spark. The other claims that it was through *his* endeavors that the material became purified, and that *he* transformed it into a vehicle for G-dliness. Each demands, "It is all mine." The ensuing discussion concerns the manner of purification to determine the reward due each disputant.

In the laws of Shabbat we find the principles of the private and public domain [in which carrying is permitted or

---

10. *Pardes* XII: 2; Tr. Expl. Notes.
11. Cf. *Maamorim* 5700-5702, "*Rebbi Omer*," 5700. Based on *Baba Metzia* 2a. [see also Hatzoat Tochen Sicha Shnayim Ochazin B'Talit, Kehot, 1996]

prohibited]. According to the inner interpretation[12] they correspond to the Four Worlds: the private domain—*atzilut*; the public domain—*briya, yetzira asiya.*

---

12. See *Likkutei Torah* of Arizal, beginning of tractate *Shabbat*. Discourse of *Mayim Rabbim* (*Torat Shmuel, Shaar* 3) chapter 3.

Chapter Thirteen

In these citations, as in all Torah law, the approach of Chasidus is of profound examination, on a completely different level than that of the Revealed Law. In the most complex of Revealed laws, affliction, sacrifice, loss, etc., the material existence of the matter around which all the intricacies of the abstract theories revolve, is tangible. Hence, the theories and principles leading to the final verdicts are relatively comprehensible. When these same laws, however, are examined by Chasidus (the obscuring of *concept* causing *nega*, the subjugation of man's powers and senses in Sacrificial Law, the "finding" of the *talit*, the domains of Shabbat), then the central point, the subject proper, is spiritual; therefore, its comprehension is far more challenging.

The "laws" around which the theories of Chasidus revolve are spiritual; even the explanations, examples, and analogies are of an abstract nature. For example, the example (above ch. 12) of *concept* and *comprehension* illustrates that when the quality of *matter* associated with *comprehension* dominates the quality of *form* associated with *concept*, the *nega* is the result, the opposite of *oneg*, delight.

When the light of the *concept*-nucleus is greater than the expansiveness of *comprehension*, the result is delight. Though *comprehension* has its intrinsic advantage (it is a state of fuller grasp of the subject than is *concept*), still the ramifications and elaboration characteristic of *comprehension* do solidify the thought. When the radiance of *concept* is greater than the expansiveness of *comprehension*, one experiences intellectual delight.

The reason for this is that *concept* is called אין *ayin*, nothingness. The revelation of *concept* in general, not only in the initial flash-revelation, comes as a "point." The delight in *concept*, delight in intellectual creativity, lies in its power of abstraction. *Comprehension* is called יש *yesh*, existence. It is manifested in its general state with breadth and expansion, like a flowing river becoming ever broader and longer, through illustrations and elucidation. In its initial manifestation, before the formulation and materialization of the thought, *comprehension* must of necessity still be described as a state of expansion. The delight in *comprehension* lies in its ability to concretize, its power of embodiment [in contrast to] *concept's* power of abstraction.

These two intellective powers are parental in their function of giving rise to emotion-attributes; the birth and revelation of emotion must be through the action of intellect. "According to his intellect is man [Hebrew איש *ish*] extolled."[1] *Ish* refers to emotional-man;[2] "extolled" implies revelation. The manifestation of emotions is in accordance with the *intellect* that gives birth to them.

Analogously, parents educate and guide their children, and they develop accordingly. Likewise, emotions, the "offspring" of intellect, develop in consonance with intellect. In the way that intellect is manifested (the direction it gives emotion) emotion will follow suit.

---

1. Prov. 12:8.
2. Cf. *On the Teachings of Chasidus*, ch. 7.

When intellect influences emotion in an orderly manner, i.e. when *concept* and *comprehension* are in proper proportion and complementary, then the emotions engendered are faultless. When the influence of intellect is disorderly and unsystematic, the emotions are correspondingly imperfect. There may be variations in the imperfection due to imbalance—whether *concept* is disproportionately dominant or *comprehension*.

This is an illustration of the approach of Chasidus to a law of afflictions. This method of interpretation is applied to all subjects of Revealed Law. Sacrificial law becomes the study of the subordination and accession of man's faculties to G-dliness; laws of found articles are examined as the service of purification of matter. Even the explanations and illustrations used in Chasidus are so abstract and spiritual as to transcend the scope of mortal intellect.

CHAPTER FOURTEEN

ALL THE FOREGOING was an explanation of Chasidus in its role
of discussing the esoteric aspects of the Revealed Law. The
Revealed aspects of these laws are clearly understood in their
detailed logic and manifold applications in practical law. Only,
it is more difficult for a person to understand the hidden aspects
of the laws with the same consummate clarity that is possible
with their Revealed aspects. But this concerns only the first
facet of Inner Torah—that which expounds and elucidates the
inner meanings of Revealed Law (above ch. 11).

Though these concepts are spiritual and delicate to the
extreme, the very fact that the Revealed aspects of the law are
comprehensible assists in understanding the esoteric aspects.
Despite the difficulties, we do have tangible points of reference
in the Revealed Law, and by dint of effort we may arrive at
thorough understanding.

The other facet of Chasidus discusses topics like creation *ex
nihilo*; permeating and encompassing light; light, life, and
power;[1] power and ability. On cursory examination, it would
seem that these subjects are devoid of concrete parallels. Let us
take an example:

We have mentioned *ayin* and *yesh*, nothingness and
existence. Regardless of mental endeavor, it remains difficult to
conceive of *nothing*. Even the first state of existence called היולי

---

1. Ibid., ch. 17, ff.

hiyuli by Nachmanides[2] has little meaning for the ordinary mind. So much more difficult is conceiving the existence of *nothing*, which is obviously the negation of existence, and that Creation derives from this non-existent. Understanding permeating and encompassing light, their differences and congruence, and understanding topics like the examples cited, which are the focus of the second facet of Chasidus, seems virtually impossible. Nonetheless, even this field of Chasidus can be fully grasped by the mind in a manner appropriate to the study.

---

2. Gen. 1:1. [*Bara*, "The Holy One created all creatures from absolute nothingness. We have no word in the Holy Tongue for the derivation of existence from non-existence except *bara* (created) . . . He brought forth from absolute nothingness a very delicate element. It has no tangibility but is a power of bringing forth, prepared to assume a form and proceed from potential to actual. It is the prime matter called by the Greeks *hyle*. After creating this prime matter He created no more, but formed and made from it. He brought everything forth from it, endowed them with forms and perfected them."]

CHAPTER FIFTEEN

IT IS A BASIC premise that intellectual activities are divided into categories that vary with the powers through which these activities are manifested. The *wisdom* (or science) of *deed* differs from that of speech, and speech from that of thought. All three—deed, speech, and thought—comprise the soul's *auxiliary-powers*, not its *essence-powers*. They are inferior in grade to emotion, and are called *garments* of the soul. The soul reveals itself and acts through them, but they are not independent entities.

Emotions, on the other hand, are *essence-powers*. They do have a sort of embodied existence (kindness, severity, mercy, etc.), but this materialization is only relative to *intellect*, which is on a higher plane of abstraction. In comparison with the *garments* though, emotions are considered *essence*.

This principle of variation is expressed, too, in the categories of intellectuals. *Chacham*, *maven*, and *daatan* vary in magnitude. The ideal, the perfection of *intellect*, is inclusiveness—*concept* containing in itself *comprehension* and *concentration*; *comprehension* containing *concept* and *concentration*, etc. Still, each of the three components of *intellect* possesses its particular, essential character. *Concept* is the original, seminal idea; *comprehension* is grasp and development of the nucleus; *concentration* is the profundity of the idea. The fulfilment of each lies in its being complemented by the others. The ideal *concept* is realized in its development and depth; *comprehension* is real when accompanied with awareness of the concept-nucleus and depth; *concentration* is perfected through the fusion of all three. Nonetheless, each retains its distinctive trait; between each of them, there is a difference in standing.

Just as differences exist in the components of the *intellect*, the instruments of ideas, so are there differences in the subjects in which the mind is engaged.

The various sciences of mechanics, art, mathematics, astronomy, medicine, the study of the soul, and the study of Torah—these are a few fields of study, all possessing obvious and unique qualities defining them. The peculiar nature of each necessitates systematic study with requisite preparations and introductions relevant to each.

By the same token, Chasidus has its own indispensable preparatory steps. With the proper introduction one may profitably engage in this study, grasping well even the most abstruse topics.

CHAPTER SIXTEEN

IN ANY FIELD of study, mastery and understanding depends on the character and method of effort expended in its study. Without question, through mental exertion one will successfully plumb the depths of wisdom. Those engaged in intellectual pursuits may be assured that through genuine, unstinting devotion, they will attain their goals.

It is written: והחכמה מאין תמצא ואי זה מקום בינה—*From* (אין) *ayin* [lit. "where"] *comes wisdom, and where is the place of understanding.*[1] The commentary *Metzudat David* explains that wisdom has no physical place-source with whose ending wisdom must end. Undoubtedly, he includes understanding in this explanation. "Where is the place of understanding," the creative sources of wisdom and understanding with whose ending their products must also end. The sources are not tangible or physical, subject to termination and destruction like physical objects. Hence, wisdom and understanding have no end.

This thought is elaborated generously in Chasidus. It is illustrated palpably to those sensitive individuals who conscientiously examine their abilities and characters, their worship and development in growth, and the awakening and illumination of their latent powers.

---

1. Job 28:12.

Thus did our holy forebears, the leaders of Chabad, broaden the path of the soul's progress until it became a highway, based on intellectual conviction and authentic and profound feeling.

CHAPTER SEVENTEEN

AMONG THE VARIOUS intellectual disciplines and the emotions, another characteristic difference is that of their proofs or verification. The most gross form of proof is that of physical tangibility, and the most subtle or delicate, that of (emotional) feeling.

The existence of a physical body is proven by its occupation of its own impenetrable space. Where a wall stands no object can pass. Its tangible and impenetrable presence testifies to its nature and existence.

Some forces act on physical bodies but lack the spatial tenancy of the physical, for example, the faculty of vision. Vision acts upon physical, space-occupying objects, and vision verifies their existence. In a flash, the scene passes into the realm of memory, and the vision-space is occupied by another sight. In turn, this one will be displaced by yet a third.

At the time of viewing, each scene occupies vision-space no less impenetrable than physical tenancy. One cannot concentrate vision on two scenes simultaneously. All the senses and powers of man are concentrated during the viewing and are affected accordingly: pleasure may ensue, or anguish. At any rate, the scene occupies "space" in all the powers of the soul, and with its disappearance another scene occupies that same space.

When one wishes to recall a scene, the scene, with all its details and the accompanying emotions aroused by it, may reappear. This indicates that the scenes are conserved in the reservoir of the memory and occupy space, comparable in its own terms to physical space. But this space is not impenetrable, since many scenes are conserved concurrently, and all may be readily recalled.

Thus, some forces act upon physical bodies, but can tolerate, without effect, coincident tenancy with other forces that act upon similar physical bodies.

CHAPTER EIGHTEEN

ANOTHER EXAMPLE. WHEN a person studies a very profound subject, concentrating all his powers, intellectual and auxiliary, no other thought penetrates his consciousness. Still, impressed on the recesses of the mind remains a topic studied earlier. Here we have an example of spiritual space, the space of the mind.

There is an example of four distinct powers that work in combination to achieve one action. Each power is clothed in the other, each directing its inferior; the lower power actuates the instructions of its superior.

In recording an idea in writing, a process ensues. First one must establish his fundamental proposition. This must then be expanded by explanation, details, and conclusions appropriate to the idea. Since the idea is to be committed to writing, it must be presented in an orderly fashion, with nothing omitted. A clarity must permeate the exposition so that it may be self-sufficient, and convey conviction no less than the exposition of an eloquent orator.

In this act of writing, four general powers combine: will, intellect, thought, and deed. *Will* directs *intellect* to delve into the idea and its component details. Through *will*, the three intellect-powers contribute to the idea. They, in turn, bring the idea into the process of thought. Through its auxiliaries (speech-in-thought and thought-in-speech)[1] appropriate verbal expressions are developed to delineate and articulate the idea, and then to vivify it through writing.

---

1. Discourse "*Ma rav tuvcha*" 5692. [Tr. Expl. Notes.]

All these three powers (will, intellect, and thought) are general, inclusive. *Will* is inclusive in that it desires the very delicate and subtle idea to be coherent even to the mediocre mind. Moreover, *will* desires that the idea be written with lucid, thorough, and precise exposition, and that *thought* discover proper articulation for the idea. *Will* is thus exercised over intellect and thought. Intellect is inclusive, since it is composed of *concept*, *comprehension* and *concentration*. *Thought* is inclusive since it contains thought-in-speech, speech-in-thought, and intellect-in-thought. In the act of writing, all three are clothed in the power of *deed*.

The process of an idea's development, in the descent from concept-source to *concept*, then to *comprehension* and *conclusion*, is accomplished through the auxiliary power of *thought*. We have just seen, in addition, that the ultimate revelation of the spiritual idea depends on the physical skill, the physical writing.

Literary ability enables the thought to be expressed lucidly and faithfully in written form, so that it comes to life. Without this ability of articulation the thought itself is amorphous. Moreover, when skilfully written, the subject is presented coherently.

Frequently, this skill can sharpen and beautify the idea far beyond its contemplative state, its state in *thought*, prior to physical verbalization.

All this demonstrates that the more a concept descends through the lower powers, the more exposition, detail, and clarity it achieves. Hence the commandment, [2] "Know this day and bring close to your hearts that the L-rd is G-d." Comprehension and knowledge are required. The oneness of the Creator, and His Unity with all creation, must actually be grasped and known.

---

2. Deut. 4:39.

CHAPTER NINETEEN

MOST OF THE SUBJECT matter of Chasidus is explained through logical parallels, drawn predominantly from the powers and faculties of the soul. Anyone with a modicum of intelligence who perseveres and studies assiduously is capable of understanding the subjects clearly, at least on the level of the illustration.

For example: the ten supernal *sefirot* parallel the ten powers of the soul. In fact, *Tanya*, chapter 3, describes the soul-powers as descendant from the ten *sefirot*. Concerning the powers of the soul, we can readily grasp the difference between the mind's intellect and the heart's emotions, and [more particularly], the variations among the components of the intellect and the various emotions. This knowledge is tangible, accessible. Through diligent intellectual exercise, one can continue to progress in comprehending the loftiest concepts.

As explained elsewhere[1] at length, there are two types of comprehension: 1) elevation of the mind to the subject studied,

---

1. *Maamorim, op. cit., Oteh Or* 5700; *HaTamim* I, p. 31.
   ["In the union of idea and thinker there are three methods:
   a. The idea, the higher, is to descend to the plane of the lower, the thinker. 'Descent' is the embodiment of the idea in illustrations and parallels so that the idea is perceptible to the thinker. This method may be compared to the one at the top of a mountain descending to be together with another at the base.
   b. The thinker, who is the inferior elevates himself to the higher, the idea. 'Elevation' is the refinement of the mind, making it capable of receiving delicate ideas. This comes through practice in abstracting the core of an idea from its illustrations in order to perceive the profundity of the unencumbered idea.

and 2) descent of the subject to the mind. Each type may be subdivided into numerous categories composed of one or both main types. Essentially, the two general approaches are "abstraction" and "embodiment." Elevation of mind is abstraction; descent of subject is embodiment.

However, the terms *abstraction* and *embodiment* are in general approximate descriptions. For each approach must include processes that are similar to those of the other.

Understanding is the result of either positive or negative reasoning. Superficially, these two processes appear to be antithetical (positive knowledge states in its terms what negative knowledge declares negatively; negative knowledge is the denial of knowing positively), but in actuality they are complementary. Positive reasoning proves the virtue of what we only know negatively; negative reasoning clarifies the positively understood. Each accentuates the virtue of the other.[2] The

---

In the first method, one strives with the idea, clothing it in explanations. It is not a different idea; it is the same idea on a lower plane, but whose proper position is on the higher plane.

In the second method, the striving is primarily with the thinker, developing the ability to abstract, to immerse oneself in the 'soul' of the idea. For abstraction one must have a powerful mind and familiarity with the processes of thought. It is a precarious path, fraught with the possibility of error. Another difficulty is that ideas lead to conclusions, and conclusions are arrived at through the medium of embodiment, whereas in abstraction the conclusion is not at all evident."]

c. the third method, not important to us here, is a synthesis of the first two.]

2. [Subjects delimited comparably to the limitations of mortal intellect (dimensional in space and time) can be understood positively, i.e. one can know what the subject is.

initial step in mastery of a subject must be the knowledge of the positive, what can be known. This applies as well to abstraction and embodiment, first one examines the embodied, or lower plane of the subject.

The first step to learning, however, is [abstraction] the elevation of the mind in the ordinary sense of the word: simply—systematic devotion to intellectual activities. In time, this will lead to the achievement of the most profound, most delicate and abstract concepts.

A supra-dimensional subject, one that transcends the limitations of mortal mind, cannot be understood in terms of what it *is*, but negatively, in terms of what it is *not*.

The complementary function of the two processes is: Positive knowledge, as far as it can be exercised, indicates the loftiness of what lies beyond its scope and can be understood only negatively (e.g. G-d is not dimensional). Negative understanding, in turn, gives clarity and definition to the positive knowledge already attained.]

Chapter Twenty

EVEN IN SECULAR studies, intellectual exercise may be either stimulating or humbling. When a person hears an idea that he can grasp and assimilate, he is stimulated to further learning, because he derives pleasure from ideas. If the idea is beyond his capacities, however, he is still affected profoundly since he can perceive the idea's loftiness. Yet, since he fails to understand the thought, he is deeply pained. But though he is humbled, he will be stirred, nonetheless, with a longing to deal competently with such ideas. Understandably, these reactions will be even more marked when dealing with G-dly concepts.

In truth, this humility is vital in intellectual pursuits. Through contriteness and humility his understanding will be clearer and more thorough, because the idea becomes all-important, and the student, more receptive. Besides, his diligence and concentration are stimulated by humility, which enable him to reach immeasurable heights.

CHAPTER TWENTY-ONE

IN THE DAYS of the Mitteler Rebbe, the knowledge of the students in the field of Chasidus was astonishing. The Rebbe had instructed all young men not burdened with earning a livelihood to study Chasidus at least three hours daily. In time, every Chasidic community boasted a growing number of youthful scholars. Later many of these young scholars became *mashpi'im* and teachers in different communities. This had a marked effect on the local Chasidim, since the study and knowledge of Chasidus promptly increased.

In the town of Lepli, there lived a Chasid of the Alter Rebbe, a salt merchant by trade, named Reb Yekusiel. He was renowned as an *oved* (his first audience with the Alter Rebbe is recorded elsewhere)[1] but his grasp of Torah, in general, and of Chasidus in particular, was extremely limited.

Once one of the young *mashpi'im* passed through Lepli and spent a week there, daily reviewing from memory a discourse of the Mitteler Rebbe. The discourses he discussed were extremely abstruse and profound. The young man was exceptionally gifted mentally and an eloquent speaker. Every word he uttered was sparkling and clear; his audience was very impressed. Reb Yekusiel, no great intellect, could not follow the discourses. He grieved bitterly and castigated himself for being so obtuse.

The famed Chasid, Rabbi Shmuel Dov of Borisov,[2] told me that Reb Yekusiel had described the incident to him. "Just

---

1. *Sicha*, 19 *Kislev* 5693, sec. 18.
2. Biography in *HaTamim* V, p. 99, ff.

imagine," Reb Yekusiel said. "I was then about forty years old. For fifteen years I had visited the Alter Rebbe, and all that time I studied Chasidus to the best of my abilities. Suddenly, something new! A stripling, a mere chick, comes repeating the Rebbe's discourses intelligently and enthusiastically; I listen and don't understand. I can feel that the topics are deep, wonderful topics, but I don't grasp a thing.

"Every day, when I heard the lad and couldn't follow, I was deeply distressed. Every discourse struck me like a hammer. I berated myself and resolved to master those discourses. I asked the lad to repeat them for me over and over again. He even did his best to interpret them for me, but my head was like a lump of wood and my brain absorbed nothing. Three weeks I kept that young man at my home. My family cared for the store while I spent days and nights on end laboring to understand what the young man taught me. To my sorrow, it did no good. He finally left and I was like a foundering ship. I fasted and prayed, but to no avail. So, I went to Lubavitch, to the Rebbe.

"For nine months, I hadn't been in Lubavitch. I found a new world there—about fifty or sixty young men devoting long hours every day to Chasidus, reviewing the discourses and explaining them to each other. I arrived in Lubavitch on a Wednesday. That Friday, before *Kabbalat Shabbat* the Rebbe delivered a discourse, and the next day before *Mincha* a *bi'ur* [elucidation] on the discourse. I grasped the discourse and could repeat parts from memory, but the *bi'ur* was beyond me. To my utter amazement, the young men understood the *bi'ur* too. I was very troubled that I couldn't grasp the *bi'ur*; I prayed all night and fasted the next day.

"On Monday I had an audience with the Rebbe. I told him all that had happened at home, the visit of the young man to Lepli, his reviews of the discourses that he had heard in Lubavitch, and that I understood the simpler ones but not those that discussed deeper subjects. I also mentioned that I had understood the discourse of Friday evening but not its *bi'ur*.

"The Rebbe replied, 'Nothing stands in the way of will.' He explained that though *will* is only a soul-power—not soul-essence—still it can control the soul to reveal the powers and senses in their essence. *Will* can certainly affect powers inferior to it, such as *intellect* and *emotion*, since it is their superior. When one truly wills, even his faculties are magnified.

"Having heard from the Rebbe that everything depends on my will, I decided to remain in Lubavitch until I would begin to understand. Through travelers by way of Lepli, I notified my family of my new plans and instructed them to operate the business in my absence. Four months I labored physically and spiritually to accustom myself to concentrate on one topic for hours without interruption, and to review a single subject scores of times. I am forever indebted to one young man, Efraim Smilianer,[3] who reviewed the discourses with me many times in succession until I was able to comprehend them. Usually I would seclude myself in the basement of the Large Synagogue or in the attic. Finally, that *Tishrei* I felt like a new man. I had 'scoured the pot' and had become a receptacle for Chasidus. I then returned home."

Before leaving Lubavitch, Reb Yekusiel had a most fascinating audience with the Mitteler Rebbe, but this is not the

---

3. *Sicha, Simchat Torah 5695*, sec. 3, ff.

occasion for discussing it. From the account of Reb Yekusiel, we can glimpse a typical old-time Chasid. When he was told in an audience that all depended on his will, he didn't budge until he corrected his deficiency, regardless of any difficulties.

My grandfather, Rabbi Shmuel, told my father, Rabbi Shalom DovBer, that the Mitteler Rebbe had divided his Chasidim into groups. Besides the general classifications of intellectuals and *ovdim* there were sub-categories. For each group he wrote special discourses and books. For one group of *ovdim* he wrote *Shaar HaTeshuva VehaTefillah* part I, for a second group, part II, and part III for a third. For one group of intellectuals, he wrote *Shaar HaEmunah*, for another *Ateret Rosh*, and for the highest group *Imrei Bina*. *Shaar HaYichud* and *Shaarai Orah* discuss general concepts and are intended for all Chasidim. *Shaar HaYichud* is the key to Chasidus, and *Shaarei Orah*, the alphabet of Chasidus.

Once my father asked my grandfather a question in *Imrei Bina*, "*Shaar Kriat Shema*," chapters 54-56, on the subject of "bread, oil, and wine" of Torah, *Secret Torah* and *Secrets of Secrets*, revealed and hidden and their intermediary. My grandfather explained fully and then said:

"*Imrei Bina* was written by the Mitteler Rebbe expressly for Reb Yekusiel Leplier. Reb Yekusiel was a clod. Though earlier he had an audience with the Alter Rebbe, and a rich one at that, still, 'you cannot place a head on an other's shoulders.' He had a sensitive heart and prayed with warmth. When the Mitteler Rebbe returned from Little Russia and settled in Lubavitch, he devoted himself to teaching the young men Chasidus. Reb Yekusiel grew envious and longed to share their knowledge. He toiled strenuously until he was capable of understanding the most abstract subjects.

"Once I couldn't understand a number of passages in *Imrei Bina*, in "*Shaar HaTefillin*," chapter 32 concerning *direct* and *reflected illumination*, and chapter 37 concerning the creation of *concept* from its source. I worked over the problems and then had an audience with my father (the "*Tzemach Tzedek*"), to whom I presented my difficulties. He referred me to Reb Yekusiel who was in Lubavitch at the time and spoke of him at length. Among other things my father remarked that *Imrei Bina* was composed for Reb Yekusiel. I was to ask *him* my questions, and then repeat his answers to my father who would elaborate.

"Reb Yekusiel habitually spent hours daily in prayer, so I requested Yosef Mordechai the attendant to notify me when Reb Yekusiel had concluded. Later, after I finally questioned Reb Yekusiel, he pondered for a while and said, 'I am a storekeeper. It is customary that before a storekeeper delivers the merchandise he receives payment. I have the merchandise. Pay the price and I will give it to you.'

"I asked him what payment he was demanding, and he answered that I review the discourse delivered that Shabbat. Whatever he didn't understand I was to explain, and what I couldn't, I was to ask my father. I agreed. He then solved my questions so clearly and systematically that I was amazed to hear such words from a man mediocre, if not actually simple, in his knowledge of Talmud. He was remarkably fluent in the profundities of Kabbalah and Chasidus, and he discussed them elaborately, with deep and broad explanations.

"When I repeated Reb Yekusiel's replies to my father, he commented, 'Reb Yekusiel is a living example of the Rabbinic saying[4] that what you seek diligently you will find. He labored much and found much.'

"That evening Reb Yekusiel came to demand the stipulated payment, and I, for my part, reviewed the discourse. He paid close attention throughout. It is unforgettable, observing an old Chasid listening to a discourse—every organ of his body listened! He asked that I be kind enough to repeat the discourse again at dawn the next morning, and I complied. At that time he presented his questions, most of which I had to refer to my father. I spent a week of utter delight with those queries and replies.

"From that time on, whenever Reb Yekusiel visited Lubavitch we spent many pleasant hours together. He distinctly remembered everything he had seen since his first visit to Liozna in the summer of 1786. He was fond of remarking, 'Every week I have an audience in my mind with the Alter Rebbe, asking him whatever I wish.' For he remembered every audience he had with the Alter Rebbe, the Mitteler Rebbe, and the *"Tzemach Tzedek."* The Alter Rebbe had blessed him with longevity and he lived almost a century."

Rabbi Shmuel Dov of Borisov extravagantly lauded Reb Yekusiel's abilities, declaring that he had never encountered so penetrating an intellect and so sharp and orderly a mind. Reb Yekusiel possessed the priceless trait of deep love for intellectual effort and no obstacle could deter him in his studies. When

---

4. *Megilla* 6b.

concentrating, Reb Yekusiel literally shut his eyes and ears and permitted nothing in the world to disturb him.

My father (Rabbi Shalom DovBer) said to me, "The narrative my father (Rabbi Shmuel) recounted to me about Reb Yekusiel's extraordinary abilities and his attainment of greatness only through tremendous personal endeavor, how he converted himself from a clod to a powerful thinker—affected me deeply in my own development."

I have elaborated at such length here to demonstrate the fact that through genuine effort one can attain incredible intellectual heights. Everything depends solely on the person himself.

CHAPTER TWENTY-TWO

IN SUMMATION: THE claim that human understanding cannot grasp Chasidus is patently false and detrimental to serving G-d. Fortunate is the person who chooses the life of studying Chasidus, the life of service through prayer, the life of labor of the mind. G-d created man with a purpose. He endowed him with mind and heart, to conceive and understand, to love and be merciful. All of one's faculties must be subordinated to His service, refining one's personality, studying Torah, service through worship, and actual performance of religious duties with inner spirit and enthusiasm.

❀

If at one time it was possible to become G-d-fearing without the knowledge or study of Chasidus, certainly in our own time, when an alien spirit pervades all segments of Jewry and libertarianism reigns unchallenged, when all parties and factions insist that the "Divine Presence speaks through their throats"— now there is no doubt that Chasidus is indispensable in teaching the Path to Life, and vital for the welfare of the soul itself.

A person who reveres the Word of G-d and who desires the good life with Divine delights—now and in the Hereafter— must fix specific periods for studying Chasidus. He must study in order to observe; to fulfill the commandment of Love of fellow Jews; and to urge his acquaintances and friends to study Chasidus and to meet regularly with his fellow Chasidim for mutual strengthening and encouragement. Thus will they "see the light that is good" and be blessed with all that is good.

Appendices

ON THE CONTRIBUTION OF CHASIDUS TO JEWISH THOUGHT AND TO A JEW'S SERVICE OF G-D

A letter by Rabbi Yosef Yitzchak Schneersohn of righteous memory. [1]

> By the Grace of G-d
> *Sivan* 27, 5696, Otwock
> (June 17, 1936)

In answer to your inquiry regarding the difference between *Musar* and Chasidus—does not *Musar* expound the vanity of the material world and the importance of Torah and religious living? What, then, does Chasidus add?

One G-d is the source of both teachings, Chasidus and *Musar*. Nonetheless there is a great difference between them. Here I will dwell on one aspect of the difference.

On the verse,[2] "Let us make man in our image, after our likeness," Rashi comments, "*In our image*—in our form; *after our likeness*—to understand and conceive [ideas]." What is meant here is that the manner of man's creation differs from that of all other creatures. Moreover, man is essentially unique in that he is modeled after the Supreme. He is endowed with intellectual gifts which other creatures lack.

---

1. This excerpt was translated by R. Zalman Posner, from *HaTamim*, vol. 6, Warsaw, 1937, p. 50-51.
2. Gen. 1:26.

159

"Beloved is man for he was created in the image of G-d [i.e. he was patterned after G-d]; an especial love was accorded to man in that it [man's uniqueness] was made known to him, that he was created in the image of G-d."[3] Through his own makeup he is enabled to conceive and understand spiritual matters.

Besides his advantage over other creatures in his being the likeness and image of G-d and possessing the ability to study Torah and G-d, he is the "central creature" that includes within himself the higher and lower creatures.

"From my flesh I see G-d."[4] From his own body and soul man can obtain a conception of G-dliness. Man is a composite of body and soul. The body in itself is called the "flesh of man"; the soul in itself is called the "soul of man"; the union of body and soul is called man. "All that G-d created in the world, He created in man,"[5] therefore man is called a "small world," a microcosm and the world is called a "large body," a macrocosm.

In this composition of body and soul, the body is secondary and the soul primary. Just as in man, the microcosm, it is the soul that is essential, not the body, so too in the world, the macrocosm, the essential component is the Divine life-force that vivifies the universe and all creatures. The physical bodies of creatures and the corporeal existence of the material world—these are all secondary.

This idea, the relative importance of the body and physical existence on the one hand, and the soul and Divine life-force

---

3. *Avot* 3:18.
4. Job 19:26.
5. *Avot d'Rabbi Natan* 31:3.

on the other, is copiously explained with elaborations and empirical proofs. With the above preface, numerous Biblical verses and Rabbinical statements can be understood.

However, this knowledge (the primacy of the soul and life-force over the material body and world) is not a single idea to be grasped in its positive and negative aspects as one. It is true that with the acceptance of the inferiority of the physical, the superiority of the spiritual follows naturally. Actually, though, they are two distinct concepts. One demonstrates the inferiority of the body, while the other discusses the soul and life-force as the essentials.

Musar and Chasidus both teach the vanity of the bodily world and the value of Torah and Torah living. The difference is that *Musar* devotes itself to the worthlessness of the physical, and Chasidus is concerned with the virtues of the spiritual. Besides, Chasidus expounds the Divine intention that physical creatures become vessels for G-dliness.

It is incumbent upon every individual to understand the importance of the Divine life-force. Every Jew must engage in this study to recognize "He Who spoke and the world came into being." At every step one must perceive Divine Providence; all one's worldly affairs must inspire his heart with love and fear of G-d, with a deep desire to fulfill G-d's plan in physical creation, namely, to make the lower world a vessel for Him.

EXPLANATORY NOTES
By Rabbi Zalman I. Posner

TERMS USED IN Chabad Chasidus are not necessarily to be understood according to their common usage. In these Notes the translator has attempted to give the specific connotation of the words in their Chabad context. The very term Chabad, an acronym for *chochma*, *bina*, and *daat*, is an example of the special meaning this system has applied to standard terms, as will be explained further in these Notes.

It must be emphasized that these Notes are not by any means a full treatment of the subject discussed. They are intended only to simplify understanding of the terms in their present context. Of necessity, the comments are frequently so brief as to merely hint at the full meaning but it is hoped that the reader will be able to follow the text with the assistance of these Notes.

SOUL-POWERS

The soul (*nefesh*) finds its expression and manifestation through its powers. There are two broad categories: 1) general powers, and 2) particular powers. The general powers are delight (*oneg*) and will (*ratzon*). They are "general" in that they are not limited to any specific part of the body. One may experience delight from, and exercise will over, the intellect, emotions, and physical organs in equal measure.

The particular powers may be subdivided into two classes, with downward progression: a) intellective powers and b) emotive powers.

INTELLECTIVE POWERS

These powers include, *chochma* (generally rendered *wisdom*, but for our purpose *concept* is preferable), *bina* (*understanding*, comprehension, intellectual grasp), and *daat* (*knowledge*, or preferably here, concentration, depth, and carrying the idea to its conclusion).

In intellectual endeavor, one may have difficulty in understanding his subject, despite all his efforts. Suddenly his mind may be illuminated with a spark, a *point*, a concept that is as yet undefined, a germ that contains within itself the solution to the problem. Because it is as yet amorphous, comprehension is lacking; the flash of illumination might indeed be dissipated unless it is promptly developed. But already the thinker experiences delight; he is aware of a great accomplishment. He is prepared to examine this concept, this *point* (comparable in its infinitesimal nature and its potential to the geometric point that is the beginning of all constructions), until he achieves perfect understanding. (This nucleus finds its source in *maskil*, the soul-power that gives rise to the intellect; *maskil* may be defined as the *intellect-source*.) In this state the concept defies articulation, it is still an abstraction, but has a degree of tangibility as compared to *maskil*. The term *concept* is used here rather than the more common renditions or *chochma*, because *concept* implies genesis of intellectual activity, creativity.

Bina takes this concept-nucleus, examines it and develops it in all its ramifications and details. The idea becomes embodied, articulate, instead of remaining abstract. The original concept-spark becomes obscured in this process, but comprehension takes its place. This development may be amplification in depth (profound understanding) or in breadth (details).

To develop properly, concept and comprehension must act in unison and balance. The obscured concept-nucleus must be evident in the expansiveness of comprehension; the breadth and depth of comprehension must be latent in the spark of concept. Exaggerated emphasis of one or the other distorts the idea and its conclusion.

Daat is the concentration and devotion to intellectual endeavor that makes possible the development of comprehension, and carries the idea to its logical conclusion. The conclusion will vary with the type of subject—a verdict in legal problems or an emotion consonant with the idea, as will be further explained.

Chochma is creative; *bina* is developmental; *daat* is conclusive. One person's forte may be *chochma*, another's *bina*, a third's *daat*. They would then be described respectively as *chochom*, *maivin* and *daatan*.

EMOTIVE POWERS

The emotive powers are the conclusions and results of the intellect-powers. Chabad Chasidus, being largely devoted to the study of G-d, insists that intellectual achievement *per se* is inadequate. The mind must carry out its conclusions in the heart (the seat of the emotions, as the brain is the seat of the intellect), in the arousal of emotions indicated by the subject under study. For example, meditation on the greatness of the Almighty might lead to fear (another term, by the way, that needs interpretation in its Chabad context, but is irrelevant to us now) of Him. Recognition of His Providence might lead to love of Him. The emotions, in turn, must affect actual deeds, that one act in the light of his understanding and feelings, continuing the unbroken sequence of mind, heart and deed. (See *On the Teachings of Chasidus*, ch. 16)

The term *Chabad* is descriptive of the principle of this school, that through systematic intellectual progression one may control, even radically alter, his emotions, and concomitantly, his deeds.

Chasidus enumerates seven emotive powers, or attributes. Since the latter four are derivative or branches of the first three, there is no need to explain them here. The first three are *chesed* (kindness), *gevura* (severity, restraint, strength), and *tiferet* (beauty).

Kindness is the inclination toward expansion, giving forth. It finds expression in charity, sharing knowledge, and simple human goodness. Love would be a corollary of this attribute, inasmuch as the characteristic of kindness creates a closeness between the parties involved.

Severity expresses itself in withholding, in limitation. Since withdrawal is a mark of severity, fear would be its corollary.

Tiferet, or beauty, is a composition of the first two, a combination of their qualities, with kindness predominating. It may be defined as *mercy*, granting where the recipient is not necessarily worthy.

Despite its attraction, kindness by itself can be corrupted and harmful. Too much bounty is not beneficial, as in the illustration of the teacher and his callow pupil (see Notes on

Condensation). Kindness must be tempered with severity, limiting the endowment to the absorptive capacity of the recipient. The merger of kindness and severity in this manner would be called *severity-in-kindness*.

Severity unmellowed is obviously undesirable. It must be alloyed with kindness, as in the denial of privilege for the purpose of improving a child. This merger, with severity basic, would be described as *kindness-in-severity*.

The other emotive-powers too are not to operate in their pristine states, but must combine with one or more of the others, according to the circumstances prevailing, according to the needs of the situation. The initial combinations result in 7x7 or 49 attributes. (See *On the Teachings of Chasidus*, ch. 29)

ENCOMPASSING AND PERMEATING LIGHT

The general powers of the soul are described as encompassing—they find their abode in no particular part of the body; they encompass all its components equally. Through its particular powers, the soul is manifested in certain vessels for each power, e.g. intellect in the brain. The soul thus permeates the body besides encompassing it. Since the particular powers are not equal in function or magnitude, it follows that there are variations in the degree of revelation of the soul in the particular vessels, or instruments, of the powers. General or encompassing powers are equally manifest in the highest parts of the body and lowest.

Chasidus describes the soul and its manifestations as parallels of G-d and His revelation. G-d encompasses creation; no distinctions of higher and lower, spiritual and material, exist. He also permeates creation, revealing Himself or concealing His presence according to the vessel or instrument of His revelation. These revelations, or illuminations, are known as encompassing light and permeating light respectively.

His encompassing light is constant, countenancing no difference between the loftiest, most spiritual being and the lowest, most gross material creature, all degrees submerged and null in the greater Light of G-d. The encompassing light is as yet unperceived by His creatures. (See explanation on *Condensation*.) However, in the permeating light, the creative power in action, He is manifested (tangibly to the sensitive) in varying degrees, and is embodied, as the life-force, within creation. The permeating light parallels the soul-powers embodied and expressed in their particular vessels of the body. Transcendent G-d could refer to His encompassing light, the supra-revelatory aspect of G-d; Providential G-d could refer to His permeating light, G-d the Creator and Master of creation.

THOUGHT AND SPEECH

The soul-powers, *intellect* and *emotion*, in turn, utilize auxiliaries or *garbs* as instruments. Intellect uses thought; emotion, of necessity existing only in terms of another external being (one fears or loves another, while relatively speaking, intellect may be purely introspective), utilizes speech. In Chabad usage then, speech implies external existence, while thought implies internal unity. Thus we speak of the vivifying *Word* of G-d, G-d creating by saying, *Let there be....*

Thought enjoys a greater unity with the soul than does speech. Its existence is not externally apparent and it is continuous in its action, whereas speech is subject to interruption. Thought does not require another being for its fulfillment, while speech can be directed only outside one's self.

Within thought there are further subdivisions. Intellect-thought describes the state of an idea existing in its pure form, to the exclusion of articulation. One first perceives an idea, then seeks its verbalization. (This applies to *comprehension*, not to *concept* alone.) In terms of expression the idea is as yet disembodied. The next step is speech-in-thought; the idea predominates but there are the beginnings of verbalization.

In thought-in-speech, the precedent to oral or scriptural articulation, the idea is systematized and expression for its presentation is developed. In this stage, speech, verbalization of the idea predominates over the abstract concept. In actual speech the idea reaches its epitome of development; it has passed the test of communication to another.

CONDENSATION

In downward progression, *tzimtzum* (condensation, contraction, concentration) is the means of orderly descent from a higher level to a lower one. When expounding an idea to his pupils, his intellectual inferiors, a teacher cannot articulate the concept in the terms of his own comprehension. He must condense his idea in such a manner (through illustrations and explanations comprehensible to his pupils) so that 1) the pupils understand, and 2) the condensed version retains all the elements of the idea in its original state.

Ultimately, by dint of acquisition of knowledge and a more highly developed mind, the student may attain the teacher's level of understanding by gradual upward progression. Without condensation of the idea, the pupil will learn nothing (the idea in its original state being beyond his capacity to comprehend) and, moreover, will become so confused as to be incapable of grasping even subjects on his own level. His mind will cease to function properly.

If the teacher's level is incomparably higher than the pupil's, if downward progression entails a radical descent, then the teacher must set aside completely the idea as he conceives it, otherwise he will fail to find terms accessible to the pupil. This first, or great condensation constitutes a complete withdrawal from the higher level; consequently, the end product (the presented idea) is infinitely lower than the original. Subsequent condensations (adaptations to the particular level of the pupil) will concern stages that have measurable relationship with each other, with no radical difference between the levels.

G-d being the Absolute Infinite, finite existence would be precluded in the process of creation (comparable to the pupil's utter confusion if presented with the teacher's original idea) without the initial great condensation. Innumerable subsequent contractions progressively conceal His infinitude, making room for the existence of physical, finite creatures. The millenial goal is the improvement and elevation of creation to the point that it be fully conscious of, and united with, the Infinite, while retaining its present character (just as the pupil attains the teacher's level without becoming the teacher).

FOUR WORLDS

The main categories of the stages of condensation are called the four worlds: *Atzilut*—Emanation, the state of proximity where He is most evident; *Briah*—Creation, a finite state radically different from its preceding infinite world; *Yetzira*—Formation, a lower state of finite existence (these three are non-physical; the latter two are subject to the limitations of spiritual beings); *Asiya*—Action, deed; this world includes our mundane world). Successively higher levels among and within the four worlds enjoy respectively higher degrees of awareness and conception of His Being.

Each of these four worlds is general; the subgradations within each may be described as *worlds* as well and are innumerable. Existences, *habitants* of the four worlds are known as *emanations*, *creatures*, etc. *Angels* in Torah refers to beings of those spiritual worlds below *Atzilut*, whose finitude may be equated with *body*. Since physical matter does not exist on those spheres, they have no physical form. The worlds are roughly analogous to the attributes—intellect and emotion—and the beings of each world are accordingly described. Hence *Abstract Intellect*—denoting the exalted plane of intellect combined with abstraction, disembodiment, superior to the dimensions of time and space.

SEFIROT

On each of the four general levels, G-d has the Divine attributes called *Sefirot* (generally rendered *spheres* or *regions*) that parallel the powers of the soul (intellect, emotion, and their components). Naturally, each *sefira* varies from world to world according to the variations of the worlds themselves.

Intellect in *Azilut* is as different from *intellect* in *Briah* as *Azilut* is different from *Briah*.

ESSENCE

Etzem, or essence, refers to the absolute, fundamental, non-derivative state of any being, the state which transcends revelation. It is non-composite. Manifestation does not involve the Essence of being, the Essence being the source of the manifestation.

Like all descriptive terms, essence has its relative and absolute meaning. (See *On Learning Chasidus*, ch. 1) It may be applied to the soul, or its components, for example, in its relative connotations. Absolute Essence can refer only to G-d; all other beings of necessity are secondary, or productions, and are not elemental. Relatively speaking, *soul-essence* refers to the soul, not its powers; *essence-powers* refers to the independent powers, not merged with the others, but in terms of the soul the powers are by no means *essence*.

TETRAGRAMMATON

G-d in His Essence-state is called by the Ineffable Name, the Tetragrammaton in Scripture, and *Havayah* in conversation. This refers to G-d the Infinite, transcending creation and nature, omnipresent and supra-temporal, precluding any existence outside Himself as an infringement on true Infinity— *There is no other* (Deut. 4:39). In order to create the mundane world He desired, He concealed His presence, He condensed His Light (see Notes on *Condensation*).

G-d as Creator is called *Elokim*, signifying limitation and the subsequent possibility of finite existence. As the teacher's condensed idea contains no elements lacking in the original from which it is derived, so too *Elokim* has no independence or qualities other than those endowed it by its source and origin, *Havayah*. As the pupil receives the condensed idea, so the finite world is called into existence by *Elokim*. *Elokim* performs the actual creation, but not of its own accord. It is, so to speak, an intermediary that brings to fruition the creative power latent, but ineluctably present, in the Infinite.

FORM AND MATTER

In the context of these pages, *form* refers to the spiritual aspect of any being, the Word of G-d that vivifies it. Form, or spirit, implies abstraction, disembodiment. *Matter*, or substance, as used here, refers to the material aspect of the being, the physical body, *body* implying tangibility.

In terms of *concept* and *comprehension* (see *On Learning Chasidus*, ch. 13), *concept* is the abstract nucleus of the idea; it has no intellectual tangibility. Even in terms of the intellect, it is spiritual. Hence the reference to *concept-form*. Comprehension—expansion and development of the nucleus —gives intellectual tangibility to the nucleus. This is the meaning of *grasp-matter*.

Chasidus teaches the pre-eminence of form-over-matter, the ideal domination of the spiritual over the physical. The reality of the being is not its physical substance, but the World of G-d, the Divine spark that gives it life, or the *form*.

COMMANDMENTS

The precepts, or *mitzvot*, of the Torah may be variously divided. There are positive commandments, e.g. phylacteries, tithes, the things we are to do. Negative commandments are prohibitions, e.g. robbery, Shabbat violation, murder, those acts we are to refrain from doing.

Some acts entail physical performance, e.g., the phylacteries are placed on the arm and head. Torah study, a religious duty, is an act of the mind. Love and fear of G-d are described as "duties of the heart."

Practical, physical duties are defined in their requirements. They may require a certain hour, or day, or time of the year for their performance. They may be dimensionally defined as to place, or size. These specifications are in time and space. Duties of the heart, though they are emotions and less prone to definition and limitation, also have qualitative and quantitative dimensions—there are degrees of love and fear every Jew is expected to attain. This difference must be noted: the requirements of the physical duties are constant, applying equally to all Jews, while the requirements of the heart duties are subjective and vary with the individual.

RABBI YOSEF YITZCHAK SCHNEERSOHN
זצוקללה"ה נבג"מ זי"ע

A BIOGRAPHICAL SKETCH[1]
By Rabbi Nissan Mindel

TO WORLD JEWRY, Rabbi Yosef Yitzchak Schneersohn, sixth Lubavitcher Rebbe, was a recognized leader and champion of Torah-true Judaism, who sacrificed himself all his life for the benefit of his people. To numerous individuals in all walks of life, he was a patriarch and sage whose word of advice and encouragement meant inspiration and comfort. To the Chabad community the world over, with its thousands of synagogues and hundreds of thousands of followers, his word was sacred and his wish a command.

His appearance was most impressive—his beard of gold and silver, his kindly eyes and majestic smile—left an unforgettable impression on all who observed him at close range. While benign and affectionate in his conversation with his numerous visitors, he could be gravely serious, fearless and outspoken, when touching upon any subject concerning the safeguarding of the religious observances or the economic improvement of his brethren, wherever they may be.

The Schneersohn Rabbinical Dynasty has for two centuries produced leadership of the rarest caliber in world Jewry. True to that tradition, the Lubavitcher Rebbe stood above party, but belonged to all Israel. Every Jew, without exception, was dear to him. Thus, while having devoted part of his time to the large

---

1 Although originally published in 1940 and subsequently updated after the passing of Rabbi Yosef Yitzchak, much of the information is current.

Chabad community the world over, with its specific problems such as the dissemination of the Chabad philosophy and the perpetuation of the Chabad tradition, much of his energies were exerted for the general economic betterment of the Jew, and the safeguarding of Judaism everywhere, to the improvement of the educational system, and the support of all Torah-true institutions regardless of affiliation.

All the beauty of Chabad scholarship and piety, loving kindness and modesty, purity of heart and faith, were personified in him. He was all that a Jewish leader should be.

His selfless devotion to his people, his self-sacrifice for Torah and Judaism, his inspiring leadership in the most critical era of Jewish history, made the sixth Lubavitcher Rebbe stand out as one of the most revered and saintly figures of the entire world of Jewry.

* * *

Rabbi Yosef Yitzchak Schneersohn was born in Lubavitch, Russia, on the 12th day of Tamuz in the year 5640 (1880). His father, Rabbi Shalom DovBer Schneersohn,[2] initiated his son into communal work at the age of fifteen, by appointing him his personal secretary.

For more than one hundred years, the Lubavitcher Dynasty enjoyed the status of privileged citizens, first granted by Czar Alexander the First, at the time of the Napoleonic invasion of Russia, in recognition of the great patriotism of Rabbi Schneur Zalman, the founder of Chabad Chasidus, and the progenitor of

---

2. 5621 – 5680 (1860 – 1920).

the Lubavitcher Dynasty. This privileged status of the Lubavitcher Rebbes in each generation (even with many non-Jews), enabled them to render invaluable service to our people in Czarist Russia.

When news of the demise of Rabbi Schneur Zalman,[3] the Alter Rebbe, reached S. Petersburg, the War Minister called a special session of the cabinet to send a message of condolence to the bereaved family.

The official address was brought to his son at Krementchug by representatives of the Governors of Poltava, Tchernigow and Odessa, with an inquiry as to the best way in which Russia could repay the Lubavitcher Rebbes for their services. The son and successor of the first Chabad leader asked nothing for himself, but requested a benevolent attitude by the Russian Government towards the Jews, and the improvement of their economic position. Asked for specific suggestions, he requested the cooperation of the government in the settling of numerous Jews on the land, a project which his father had taken up just before the Franco-Russian war broke out. Thus the famous Jewish settlements of Kherson came into being.

The Settlement expanded, and to thousands of Jewish families it meant nothing less than salvation.

The grandson of Rabbi Schneur Zalman, the world famous Talmudist and codifier, author of *"Tzemach Tzedek,"* Rabbi Menachem Mendel of Lubavitch,[4] third generation of Lubavitcher Rebbes, acquired whole tracts of land around the

---

3. 24 *Tevet* 5573 (1812).
4. 5549–5625 (1789–1866).

town of Shtzedrin, including the town itself, where new Jewish settlements were established.

These efforts were further developed by each generation of Chabad leaders, right up to the time of Rabbi Yosef Yitzchak Schneersohn, when the *American Joint Distribution Committee* began to take an active interest in Russia's farming projects.

The settling of many Jews on farms was by no means the only activity which occupied the Lubavitcher Rebbes, with the purpose of alleviating the terrible economic plight of the Jews in Russia and Poland. They propagated the idea of artisanship among Jews, and raised their standards, economically and socially, to a place of recognition in Jewish life. No longer were Jewish artisans looked upon as the dregs of society. The son of the *"Tzemach Tzedek"* had induced the government to grant them special privileges of domicile in restricted areas, on a par with Jewish businessmen and professionals. The Lubavitcher Rebbes worked for the establishment of schools for training Jewish artisans. They also endeavored to create labor and occupation for Jewish workers, such as the establishment of the famous textile factory in Dubrovna, through the initiative of the father of Rabbi Yosef Yitzchak Schneersohn.

The Lubavitcher Rebbes were the true champions of Russian Jewry, always defending its economic positions against the restrictions and discriminations imposed upon the Jews by one government decree after another. Whether it was the annulment or postponement of an expulsion decree, such as in the years 1853-57 in the district of Vohlyn, or in the year 1891 in Moscow; or in the decree depriving Polish Jews of the right of running breweries in the year 1860, or the fight against the waves of pogroms and the like, the Lubavitcher Rebbes carried the fight fearlessly and selflessly to the highest spheres of the Russian Government and Court, and to the attention of the civilized world abroad, when it became necessary.

It is beyond the scope of this brief biography to enlarge upon the accomplishments of the earlier generation of the Lubavitcher Rebbes. The above brief references were made merely to give the reader a better insight into the position that the Lubavitcher Rebbe holds, not merely as leader of the Chabad world, but of world Jewry in general.

* * *

As personal secretary to his illustrious father, the young Rabbi Yosef Yitzchak Schneersohn participated in all important Rabbinical convocations, political conferences, and the sundry other public activities of his father. In 1895, soon after he had joined his father in his public work, he participated in the great conference of religious and lay leaders which took place in Kovno, and the following year in Vilna.

On the 13th day of *Elul* 5657 (1897), at the age of seventeen, Rabbi Yosef Yitzchak married Nechamah Dinah, daughter of Rabbi Abraham Schneersohn, a prominent man of great scholarship and piety. During the week's celebration that followed the wedding ceremony, his father, Rabbi Shalom DovBer, announced the founding of the famous Lubavitcher Yeshiva Tomchei Tmimim, and the following year, appointed his son executive director. Under the able direction of Rabbi Yosef Yitzchak, and guided by his ever watchful father, the Lubavitcher Yeshiva flourished and opened many branches in various parts of the vast expanses of Russia.

In the strenuous efforts of his father to improve the economic status of the Jews in Russia, Rabbi Yosef Yitzchak Schneersohn was delegated by his father to carry on an intensive campaign for the establishment of a textile factory in Dubrovna. This campaign, which was conducted in the year 1901, took Rabbi Yosef Yitzchak to Vilna, Brisk, Lodz and Koenigsberg.

With the cooperation of the leading Rabbis of that time, including Rabbi David of Karlin, Rabbi Eliah Chaim of Lodz, Rabbi Chaim of Brisk, and Rabbi Chaim Ozer of Vilna, as well as the famous philanthropists, the brothers Jacob and Eliezer Poliakoff, a large textile factory was established in Dubrovna, in the district of Mogilev, giving employment to numerous Jewish workers, supporting some two thousand persons in all.

The difficult position of the Jews under the Czarist regime need not be elaborated upon here. As mentioned before, however, the Lubavitcher Rebbes continually interceded on behalf of their brethren, both with the government and the court. Such intercessions took Rabbi Yosef Yitzchak to the capital of S. Petersburg many times, as well as to Moscow. His visit to the capital in the year 5662 (1902) proved highly successful.

When the Russo-Japanese War flared up in the Far East in 1904, Rabbi Yosef Yitzchak became quite active in the campaign inaugurated by his father to provide the Jewish soldiers on the far eastern front with *matzot* for Pesach.

The widespread unrest that followed in the wake of that war, known as the October Revolution, its suppression and the wave of pogroms that swept the Pale of Settlement, once again spurred his father into determined action. The Rebbe was sent to Germany and Holland, where he conferred with prominent statesmen, and induced them to intercede on behalf of the persecuted Jews in Russia, in order to suppress the wave of pogroms there. These efforts, too, proved highly successful.

In the year 5668 (1908), Rabbi Yosef Yitzchak again participated in the Rabbinical convocation which took place in Vilna. In the following year, he went to Germany to confer with Jewish leaders there. Upon his return he took part in the preparation for the next Rabbinical convocation in the year 5670 (1910).

His energetic and far-reaching public activities, his watchful defense of the rights of the Russian Jew, and his constant fight against local and central authorities aroused the displeasure of the then Czarist regime. During the ten years between 5662 and 5671 (1902–1911), Rabbi Yosef Yitzchak was arrested in Moscow and S. Petersburg no less than four times.

Since governmental inquiries could find nothing incriminating in the Rebbe's activities, he was released each time, with a stern warning which, nevertheless, did not deter him from continuing his work on behalf of his people with ever-growing vigor. In the years 1917 and 1918 Rabbi Yosef Yitzchak again took a leading part in the convocations of Rabbis and laymen in Moscow and Kharkov.

* * *

The time came when Rabbi Yosef Yitzchak, upon his father's death on the second day of *Nissan* 5680 (1920), was left alone to assume full responsibility of leadership. At the request of the entire Chabad world, Rabbi Yosef Yitzchak accepted the leadership as Lubavitcher Rebbe.

By that time conditions had greatly changed. Russia was being bled white in the wake of war, revolution and constant internal strife, and, as usual, the Jews were the greatest victims. In those days, the Rebbe found himself practically alone, facing a task that required superhuman effort. He began to work on the rehabilitation of the Jewish communal and religious life in Russia. His fight was on two fronts. The material position of the Jews had been reduced to the lowest degree of poverty and suffering, and the future of traditional Judaism was gravely threatened by the policy of the godless Jewish group known as the *Yevsektzia*.[5]

While single-handedly pitted against overwhelming odds in his fight for the preservation of traditional Judaism in Russia, the Rebbe realized that the great Torah center of Russia was destined to move to a new country. Therefore, he founded a Lubavitcher yeshiva in Warsaw, Poland in the year 5681, and helped many students and deans of his Russian yeshivot to make their way to Poland to carry on with the growing Lubavitcher yeshiva there.

The Lubavitcher yeshiva in Poland, like its forerunners in Russia, rapidly developed into a whole system of yeshivot with many branches in which hundreds of students were enrolled.

In the meantime, the Rebbe, Rabbi Yosef Yitzchak Schneersohn fearlessly conducted his work in Russia,

---

5. Notorious anti-religious organization, eventually dissolved by the Soviet Government.

establishing and maintaining yeshivot and Torah schools, and other religious institutions in various parts of the country. He ignored the warnings and threats of the *Yevsektzia*. At that time, the Rebbe had his center in Rostov-on-the-Don, but because of libelous accusations, he had to move. He took up residence in Leningrad (S. Petersburg) from where he relentlessly continued to direct his activities. At that time, he also organized a special committee to help Jewish artisans and workers who desired to observe the Shabbat. He sent out teachers and preachers and other representatives to the most remote Jewish communities in Russia to strengthen their religious life. In many instances, the Rebbe supported Rabbis and institutions through loans and subsidies, as it was very difficult to organize financial help in those days.

The Lubavitcher Rebbe found it necessary at that time to organize Chabad communities outside of Russia. It was then that *Agudas Chasidei Chabad of the United States of America and Canada* was organized, and he established regular contact with his followers in the New World.

In 1927, the Rebbe founded the Lubavitcher yeshiva in Bukhara, a remote province of Russia.

His fight against those who wanted to undermine the Jewish religion and religious observance became ever more bitter. The *Yevsektzia* was determined to stop him. They resorted to intimidation and mental torture. An illustration in point is the following:

One morning, while the Rebbe was observing *yahrzeit* after his father, three members of the secret (now defunct) *Tcheku* rushed into his synagogue, guns in hand, to arrest him. Calmly

rushed into his synagogue, guns in hand, to arrest him. Calmly he finished his prayers and then followed them. Facing a council of armed and determined men, the Rebbe once again reaffirmed that he would, under no threat of compulsion, give up his religious activities. When one of the agents pointed a gun at him, saying, "This little toy has made many a man change his mind," the Rebbe calmly replied: "Your little toy can intimidate only a man who has many gods (passions) and but one world (this world). Because I have only one G-d and two worlds, I am not impressed by your little toy."

* * *

This relentless struggle, however, came to a head in the summer of the year 1927, when the Rebbe was arrested and placed in solitary confinement in the notorious Spalerno Prison of Leningrad. The Rebbe's life was now in imminent danger, but thanks to timely intervention by leading foreign statesmen, his life was spared. The intervention came in the nick of time, as a death sentence had already been passed.[6]

For some time the Rebbe was banished into exile at Kostroma in the Urals. Finally, again giving way to great pressure by prominent foreign statesmen, the authorities released the Rebbe on his birthday, Tamuz the 12th-13th, and he was permitted to settle in the village of Malachovka, in the vicinity of Moscow. Further intercession resulted in permission for the Rebbe to leave Russia and come to Riga, Latvia. On the day after Succot, the Rebbe left for Riga, together with his family and the bulk of his valuable and historic library.

---

6. For a detailed account, see **The Heroic Struggle** (Kehot, Brooklyn, 1997)

Without pausing to rest, the Rebbe renewed his activities. He began by establishing a yeshiva in Riga. In the years 1928–9, he took the initiative in providing Russian Jews with *matzot*. His efforts were highly successful.

In the year 1929, the Rebbe visited Israel and from there, traveled to the United States. Here he received an official civic welcome in New York, and was granted the freedom of the city by the Commissioner of Police, acting on behalf of the Mayor. Hundreds of Rabbis and lay leaders welcomed the Rebbe and sought personal audiences. During this visit, the Rebbe was also received by President Hoover at the White House.

Returning to Europe he continued his varied activities, and in order to have better facilities for his work, he took up residence in Warsaw (5694) 1934. The activities of the Lubavitcher yeshivot in Poland now gained considerable momentum. The central yeshiva in Warsaw and Otvock attracted many hundreds of scholars from all parts of Poland and other countries, including the United States. Two years later the Rebbe moved to Otvock, near Warsaw, and from there directed all his activities.

Storm broke out again, in September, 1939, with Europe in the throes of a second world war. Refusing every opportunity to leave the inferno of Warsaw until he had taken care of his yeshivot, and done everything possible on behalf of his suffering brethren in the Polish capital, the Rebbe remained there throughout the terrible siege and bombardment of Warsaw, and its final capitulation to the Nazi invaders. His suffering during this time, and his narrow escape under terrific bombardment, were not, however, in vain.

this time, and his narrow escape under terrific bombardment, were not, however, in vain.

He had managed to evacuate a great many of his students to safer zones, and all the American boys who had been studying at the Lubavitcher yeshiva at Otvock were safely transported back to their homes in the United States. His courage and fearlessness (he had a *succah* built and observed the *mitzvah* of "dwelling in the *succah*" at the height of the bombardment) were a source of inspiration to the suffering Jewish community of Warsaw.

It was only after he realized that there was nothing more that he could do that the Rebbe finally consented to heed the urgent requests of his many followers in Warsaw and abroad, particularly in the United States, to leave the shattered and charred ruins of the Polish capital, and make his way to the United States. The Rebbe's ardent followers and friends in America, through the cooperation of the United States Department of State in Washington, worked incessantly to facilitate the Rebbe's transportation from Warsaw to New York. Finally, the Rebbe and his family were offered transportation to Berlin, and thence to Riga, Latvia.

Riga, the capital of Latvia, which was still neutral at that time, offered further opportunity for the Rebbe to help the numerous refugees, who had succeeded in escaping from Poland to Lithuania and Latvia, among them many students and Rabbis.

On the 9th day of *Adar* II, 5700 (19 March 1940), the Rebbe arrived in New York on the SS. *Drottingholm*, and was enthusiastically welcomed by thousands of followers and many

Immediately upon his arrival, the Rebbe publicized that it was not for his own safety that he had made the trip to the United States, but that he had an important mission to fulfill in this free and blessed country. This mission was to make America a Torah center to take the place of the ruined Jewish communities of Europe.

The decade that had elapsed between the Rebbe's first and second visit to the U.S.A. left its scar on the Rebbe's constitution. His health had greatly deteriorated by his suffering and self-sacrifice. Nevertheless, the Rebbe threw himself at once, body and soul, into his new mission.

The central Yeshiva Tomchei Tmimim, Lubavitch, was soon established, and it became the forerunner of many yeshivot and Torah schools throughout the United States. The Rebbe continued his efforts on behalf of his war-torn brethren overseas, and at the same time, concentrated every ounce of energy on behalf of American Jewry, to bring about a religious revival here.

After a short stay in Manhattan, the Rebbe moved his headquarters to Brooklyn. The first issue of the monthly journal *Hakriah Vehakdusha* made its appearance as the official organ of the *World Agudas Chasidei Chabad*.

The Rebbe then founded the *Machne Israel, Inc.* and *Merkos L'Inyonei Chinuch, Inc.* organizations. The first is devoted to the general strengthening of Orthodox Judaism in America and the world over, and the other is dedicated to every phase of Jewish education, including the establishment and maintenance of many schools for girls; the publication of text-books and literature; the organization of Jewish youth into religious observance groups and circles, and so forth. These institutions are not Chabad institutions, *per se*, but are devoted to the general objective of strengthening Judaism and the remedying of the general position of Jewish education, consonant with the policy of the Lubavitcher Rebbes in the past five generations. The *Kehot Publication Society* was the next organization established. To head the three latter organizations, the Rebbe appointed his son-in-law, and future leader of Chabad-Lubavitch, Rabbi Menachem M. Schneerson.

* * *

The aims of the *Machne Israel* and *Merkos L'Inyonei Chinuch* organizations are dedicated to the welfare of all Jews without distinction. The idea of *Ahavat Yisrael* (love of fellow Jews), which permeates the work of these organizations, does not allow any distinction between one Jew and another, where Jewish spiritual and material welfare is concerned. Through the dissemination of literature in the spirit of our Torah and prophets of old, through the distribution of religious articles, support of religious institutions, and so on, the *Machne Israel* organization has brought new vitality and meaning to thousands of Jews in every walk of life.

Of course, special attention was given to Jews in the armed services, and a wave of religious re-awakening swept the rank and file of the Jews at home and abroad, the like of which had been unknown and held impossible here in America.

An eloquent illustration of the activities of these two organizations under the auspices of Rabbi Yosef Yitzchak Schneersohn was the Farmers' Department of these organizations. This department sent a special representative by car to visit the Jewish farmers in the States of New York, New Jersey, Connecticut and Massachusetts. Words can hardly describe what this visit meant to those lonely farmers. For many decades they had come to regard themselves as forsaken and forgotten. Most of them had become completely estranged from Judaism. Their children would almost certainly have been lost to us forever. Now direct contact was made with these 'lost tribes of Israel.' The above mentioned organizations furnished them free of charge, or at cost price, with various essential religious articles, fine literature and textbooks to make them conscious and proud of their great spiritual heritage.

The publication department of *Merkos L'Inyonei Chinuch* has published millions of volumes of various publications, including Hebrew textbooks, juvenile library editions, two monthly journals, various pamphlets and booklets and other literature in Hebrew, Yiddish, English, French and Spanish. Who can estimate the far reaching moral effect of these publications on our growing Jewish youth, who until now have been fed on literature completely alien to the Jewish spirit?

Thousands of children of the Public Schools in greater New York and in other cities now receive religious instruction every week through the initiative and services of the *Merkos L'Inyonei Chinuch*, taking advantage of the provision of the Education Department releasing all students for one hour a week for religious instruction. It has also mobilized a legion of voluntary instructors from the ranks of senior yeshiva students to conduct these special religious classes. Special literature and pedagogic instruction are given to these teachers to conduct the classes in the best possible way.

Thus, not merely are thousands of Jewish children brought back to the Jewish fold, but through them the light and warmth of Judaism gradually penetrates into their homes.

Not of less importance is the work of the *Merkos L'Inyonei Chinuch* in the field of *chinuch habanot*—girls' education. Girls' schools under the name of *Bais Sarah* and *Bais Rivkah* have been established by this organization in New York and throughout the continent, including Canada, as well as in the Holy Land, England, France, Morocco and Australia. There are now several hundred such schools, in which thousands of Jewish girls are educated.

Hundreds of *Mesibos Shabbos* groups, for boys and girls, have been established by the same organization from coast to coast, whereby Jewish children and youths are made conscious of their great spiritual heritage. Meeting every Shabbos in a congenial atmosphere, led by a boy, or a girl—depending on the group— of their own age, these children become aware of the fundamentals of the Jewish religion, of the sanctity of the Shabbat and other precepts. They form a potential reservoir for yeshivot and Talmud Torahs.

At the end of the war, in 1945, when so many thousands of Jews were suffering in the DP camps of Europe and clamoring for help, Rabbi Yosef Yitzchak established the *Ezrat Pleitim Vesidurom*, his *Refugee Relief and Rehabilitation Organization*, with a special office in Paris. Concentrating his efforts on this work, and with the help of the Almighty, the Rebbe succeeded in saving many hundreds of his own students and disciples and other Jews, from Russia, Poland, Lithuania, Latvia, etc., and in rehabilitating them in various countries as Rabbis and teachers, or in various professions, trades and businesses.

Many of these Jewish refugees came to Israel through the help of the *Ezrat Pleitim*, and in 1948, the Rebbe established Kfar Chabad, near Tel Aviv, where many refugees settled down to agricultural work. The village has made excellent strides in its development and is a model of dedication and industriousness. It has its own religious institutions, including a yeshiva. In recent years vocational schools have been established there, such as an agricultural school, a school for carpentry, and a school for printing. A second Chabad village, in the vicinity of the first, is being established.

A short while before his death, Rabbi Yosef Yitzchak turned to his followers and supporters with the following message: "There is much to be done in North Africa. The Jews of Morocco need teachers and guides, and it is our task to spread the knowledge of Torah among them."

This message resulted in the campaign for Jewish education and Torah-learning in Morocco. At present, many schools, teacher's seminaries, yeshivot and Talmud Torahs have been established in the various cities and towns of Morocco and in other parts of the world. All of these institutions and organizations for children, boys and girls, bear the name *Oholei Yosef Yitzchak Lubavitch*, in memory of the one who had conceived of this work, the sixth Lubavitcher Rebbe, Rabbi Yosef Yitzchak Schneersohn, of saintly memory.

The achievements in the field of Jewish education and the general strengthening of Judaism here in America which can be credited to the Rebbe's direct or indirect influence, clearly prove the old Jewish axiom: *Nothing can stand in the way of a determined will.*

In many quarters, the Rebbe removed the handicap which has more than anything else been responsible for the deplorable state of Judaism and Jewish education in America. The handicap was the common belief that *America is different*, and that *America is not suitable to become a center for Torah and G-d-fearing Jews.*

The Rebbe constantly underscored that strict adherence to the Torah as a factor in Jewish life is not limited to any particular country or any special conditions of time and place. He further impressed upon all our people, by word and by deed, that no matter how estranged a Jew may be from Torah—Judaism , the Jewish heart and soul remain unaffected, and the Jew can always be made aware and conscious of his or her great spiritual heritage, provided the right approach is taken.

Many Jewish communal workers and leaders have taken heart in the Rebbe's successful efforts, and redoubled their own. New organizations and institutions have sprung up in the field of Jewish education, Shabbat observance, etc., the benefit of which is making itself increasingly felt.

Paraphrasing the words of the wisest of all men (Proverbs 10:25) וצדיק יסוד עולם—it can truly be said that Rabbi Yosef Yitzchak, was one of the foundations of world Jewry in his generation.

Rabbi Yosef Yitzchak Schneersohn passed away on Shabbat, the 10th day of *Shevat*, 5710 (1950), after thirty years of indefatigable leadership as head of Chabad and as leader of world Jewry, of which the last ten years were spent in dedicated work from his headquarters in Brooklyn, New York.

News of his demise saddened Jews all over the world, who mourned with a sense of personal loss the passing of so eminent, devoted and inspiring a leader. However, they found comfort not only in the knowledge that his spirit lives on in the unbroken chain of Chabad leadership, but also in the fact that his deeds and institutions continue to thrive under the leadership of his successor, the seventh Lubavitcher Rebbe and head of Chabad, Rabbi Menachem Mendel Schneerson [of righteous memory.]

FOUNDERS OF CHASIDISM
AND LEADERS OF CHABAD-LUBAVITCH

THE FOUNDER OF CHASIDISM
Rabbi Yisrael Baal Shem Tov
Elul 18, 5458—Sivan 6, 5520 (1698-1760)

SUCCESSOR
Rabbi DovBer, the Maggid of Mezritch
(Date of birth unknown)—Kislev 19, 5533 (?—1772)

FOUNDER OF CHABAD
Rabbi Schneur Zalman of Liadi, the "Alter Rebbe"
Elul 18, 5505—Tevet 24, 5573 (1745-1812)

SECOND GENERATION
Rabbi DovBer of Lubavitch, the "Mitteler Rebbe"
(Son of Rabbi Schneur Zalman)
Kislev 9, 5534—Kislev 9, 5588 (1773-1827)

THIRD GENERATION
Rabbi Menachem Mendel, the "Tzemach Tzedek"
(Grandson of R. Schneur Zalman; son-in-law of R. DovBer)
Elul 29, 5549—Nissan13, 5626 (1789-1866)

FOURTH GENERATION
Rabbi Shmuel Schneersohn
(Son of Rabbi Menachem Mendel)
Iyar 2, 5594—Tishrei 13, 5643 (1834-1882)

FIFTH GENERATION
Rabbi Shalom DovBer Schneersohn
(Son of Rabbi Shmuel)
Cheshvan 20, 5621—Nissan 2, 5680 (1860-1920)

SIXTH GENERATION
Rabbi Yosef Yitzchak Schneersohn
(Son of Rabbi Shalom DovBer)
Tammuz 12, 5640—Shevat 10, 5710 (1880-1950)

SEVENTH GENERATION
Rabbi Menachem Mendel Schneerson
(Son-in-law of Rabbi Yosef Yitzchak;
Sixth in direct paternal line from Rabbi Menachem Mendel)
Nissan 11, 5662—Tammuz 3, 5754 (1902-1994)